The place is England and the time is July 1087, nearly twenty-one years after the Battle of Hastings, the start of the Norman Conquest. Re-creating one typical day in this last summer of William the Conqueror's reign, Alfred Duggan gives a meticulous, spirited account of the lives of the children of a Norman baron and a Saxon land-owner, the children of peasants and a London family, and boy novices in a cloister. He describes the details of their daily life—food, clothing, houses, travel—and shows us what it was like to live at a time when two cultures, Norman and Saxon, were struggling to adapt to each other.

Alfred Duggan

Growing Up with the
Norman Conquest

ILLUSTRATED BY C. WALTER HODGES

Pantheon Books

CONTENTS

GROWING UP
WITH THE
NORMAN
CONQUEST

I · THE FAMILY
OF A NORMAN BARON

It is July in the year 1087, nearly twenty-one years after the Battle of Hastings. William the Conqueror has been King of England since he was crowned in Westminster Abbey on Christmas Day 1066, and everybody here in Sussex is quite sure he will die on the throne, to be succeeded by some member of his family. They do not yet know that he will die before winter; for on this very day he will be thrown against the saddle of his plunging horse and injured internally, as he rides through the burning ruins of Mantes. He had plenty of time to arrange for the future of his realm, since he lingered, mortally sick, until the following September.

On this fine July morning everyone in the Sussex castle rises early, at sunrise if not before. A subdued bustle is already beginning in the kitchen as the watchman takes the banner from its nook under the stairs, plants it in a socket on top of the tower, and blows his horn as a signal that day has come.

The castle is the main residence of the lord Richard fitzRichard, the capital of his "Honor." That is the name for the collection of manors that make up his barony. Some of these manors lie near York and others on the Welsh border, but everyone who has business with his chancellor must travel to Sussex.

In centuries to come the castle will develop into a fine stone building, whose ruins impress the twentieth-century sightseer; but in 1087 it is still a field fortification, run up in a few weeks while Duke William and his army were marching on London after the Battle of Hastings. The sides of a little chalk hill about forty feet high were dug away with spades, leaving a pudding-shaped mound just too steep for a horse to scramble up. The flat top, less than an acre, is surrounded by a tall palisade. Within the palisade are a well, a few wooden sheds to house the store of emergency rations, and a small square tower of timber and stone, just tall enough to show over the wall. Within this tower is the guardroom, and on its roof the watchman has just planted his banner.

The mound is the *motte*, in a military sense the most important part of the castle. But in peacetime as few people as possible live on this cramped windy plateau. From the top of the mound a pathway has been built out, at a slope convenient for horses, leading down to the main living quarters, the bailey. This is an enclosure, much bigger than the *motte*, defended by a palisade and ditch. Within it are various buildings of timber: a hall, a separate kitchen, a bower for the ladies, cabins for the soldiers of the garrison and for the servants. The hall is carefully painted and carved, meant to last; the other buildings are no more permanent than army huts of the present day. They are made and destroyed as they are needed; in a castle there will always be enough carpenters and laborers for work of this kind.

This bailey, a well-defended enclosure, lies on one side only of the *motte*. During a siege it can be covered by archers stationed on the *motte*, but if things go badly all the defenders may retire to the top of the steep mound, where they can hold out for as long as their provisions last. A *motte* cannot be stormed without heavy loss of life.

On this July morning the lord Richard, a wealthy baron and a personal friend of the King, is absent with the main army in France. But the castle shelters a great number of people, including his family. In command is his wife, the lady Gunhild. She has been sleeping in the bower, in her great carved marriage-bed. The bower is partitioned into two rooms, and in the other room sleep her ladies and her daughter Matilda. Matilda is ten years old.

In lesser wooden cabins sleep the knights of the garrison, a few young boys, and the lady Gunhild's two sons, Robert, aged twelve and William, aged eight. These two brothers and their sister are all the surviving children of the family; four others were born, but they died in infancy.

As soon as they are awakened by the horn all the men and boys in these cabins get up and begin to dress. They are frightfully crowded together, as crowded as emigrants in a ship. In a sense this castle is very like a ship, a place where a garrison of Normans may sleep safe amid a surrounding sea of English. But at this point we must remember that they never speak of themselves as Normans. Invariably they call themselves French. When the King issues a proclamation it is addressed to "all his men, French and English." When an unexplained corpse is found in a public place (which happens far too often) the first question the neighbors must answer is: Was this dead man French or English? There is no Norman language; all Normans speak French. Only very occasionally, when encouraging troops before battle, will some leader boast that Normans fight better than other kinds of Frenchmen.

The army which conquered at Hastings was French, not Norman. The knights and barons of Normandy at first refused to follow their duke to England, explaining that they were bound to defend his duchy but not to win kingdoms for him. In the end most of them came, as volunteers or mercenaries; but so did a number of knights from other parts of France. Before the battle William drew up his line in three more or less equal divisions—Bretons, Normans, other Frenchmen. So a great many of the families which "came over with the Conqueror" did not start from Normandy.

As a young and landless knight the lord Richard charged at Hastings. Immediately afterwards he was rewarded with a good slice of Sussex. Since then he has remained unswervingly loyal to his lord, so that now after all the later rebellions and civil wars he has become one of the barons of England, one of fewer than two hundred great men with an unchallenged seat on the King's Council.

All his land was given to him by King William, and he owes service to King William for it. But he and the King do not think of his title to this land in exactly the same way. William sees himself as the rightful successor of King Edward the Confessor, nearest in blood through Queen Emma—Edward's mother and his own great-aunt —and chosen by his predecessor to be heir. He rules England by the same right and under the same laws as King Edward; it just so happens that he has been troubled by rebellion and has rewarded faithful followers with land confiscated from defeated traitors.

The lord Richard, on the other hand, remembers that long ago he risked his life in a successful co-operative enterprise, the conquest of England. For this he received the share of English land which had been promised to all successful invaders. William rules, not because King Edward named him heir, but because a gallant army put him on the throne. If he should turn against this gallant army, which God forbid, the knights might justly choose another leader. Normans do not think of their Duke William as possessing the almost sacred aura of kingship.

The castle is primarily a military encampment, and no one lingers in bed after the horn has blown. Robert and William have thrown off their blankets and jumped up stark naked, for in bed they wear no clothing. At once they begin to dress.

The first garments they put on are long linen drawers cut like jodhpurs, loose to the thigh and tight from knee to ankle. A strap under the instep keeps them from working up, and a string around the waist keeps them from slipping down. These breeches, or *braies*, are put on at once because nakedness is considered uncouth and degrading. Linen is expensive, and the boys wear no other underclothes at all; their less wealthy companions wear *braies* also, for decency, but made of wool.

Thus covered, all the boys and young men run out to wash at the trough in the court. They wash in cold water, without soap. But they keep their faces and hands pretty clean all the same, because it is socially disgraceful to be grimy or smelly. The baron's sons have their own private towels, hanging on pegs beside the trough. Others scramble for the public towels; there are seldom enough to go round.

Then comes the serious business of dressing; serious not because they wear splendid clothes but because everything must be neatly arranged. On top of a white woolen shirt each boy puts a tunic on over his head. The tunic reaches to the knees and is made of fine blue cloth; its sleeves are wrist length and so narrow that the hands can barely be squeezed through. Round the tunic runs a narrow leather girdle, but it cannot be seen, for the upper part of the tunic is pulled over it to make a handy pouch for odds and ends.

That is enough for warmth and decency. Now come the ornamental embellishments. Each boy winds long woolen puttees from ankle to just below the knee. They must be wound symmetrically and evenly, a tedious job. But these crisscross leg bandages are the mark of every well-dressed man, as are in our own day a clean collar and a neat tie.

Their shoes also are elegant: close-fitting and made of soft leather. A slit over the instep is fastened with a buckle, so there are no laces which might dangle. When all this has been done properly no glimpse of the *braies* appears below the knee.

Before appearing in public, Robert combs his hair. He combs it back from a center parting; he wears it rather longer than most of us do nowadays, but it does not quite touch his shoulders. William, who is younger and very busy being tough, has his hair cut short on the crown and clipped as close as possible below the ears. When he is old enough to be shaved he intends to have the back of his neck shaved also, to make his head more comfortable under the helmet. Neither of them wears any headdress, nor does any other man inside the castle. Only for a winter journey would a knight put on a cap or a hood.

All this has been done very quickly, for fear they should keep their mother waiting. Next they fold their straw mattresses and their thick woolen blankets. They have no other bedding. For a pillow any soft bundle of clothes will do; linen sheets are too expensive for boys. William fastens his scabbarded knife to his girdle, Robert slips his inside the bosom of his tunic. That is all they carry with them; they never use a handkerchief and seldom use money.

Although they have hurried they are only just in time to attend morning prayers in the hall. One of the clerks who works in the castle is a priest, and somewhere in the tower is a consecrated altar stone, thin and easily carried on horseback. But there is no chapel, and they do not hear Mass every weekday.

Yet morning prayers are a considerable ceremony. The priest stands before a lectern to read from a handsome psalter the psalm for the day. The servants and the common foot soldiers of the garrison kneel in a dense mass at the back of the room. The gentry take up more space, for they lie decorously face down on the floor, arms stretched out in the form of the Cross. They mutter some familiar prayers in unison, but of course they cannot join in what the priest reads from his book. None of them has a private psalter of his own.

While Robert prays he makes up his mind once again that when he inherits this castle he will build a proper chapel and hear Mass every day, as a great baron should. Father would have arranged that long ago, except that he is so seldom at home. Everyone prays with genuine devotion. A civilized man ought to give a reasonable time daily to God. In this fallen world you have to do various unpleasant things to your enemies to prevent them from doing even worse to you and your family. It would be better if you could keep all the Commandments all the time. But since obviously you cannot, the next best thing is to pray frequently for forgiveness.

When prayers are finished the boys greet their mother and sister. The lady Gunhild is dressed for a quiet day in the country. Over the plain linen smock which is her only undergarment is a long kirtle, put on over the head and reaching to the ground. On top of that she wears a super-tunic of very much the same shape, except that its loose sleeves fall back to the elbow to display the long tight sleeves of the kirtle. On her head is a white woolen ker-chief, covering all her hair and crossed under the chin to frame her face. Her shoes of soft leather are like a man's. Her legs are hidden, but on them she wears long stockings of colored cloth, fastened above the knee by woolen garters. The cloth of the stockings is meant to fit tightly, but knitting has not yet been invented.

Matilda dresses like her mother, in smock, kirtle, super-tunic, and stockings. But because she is still a child her hair hangs down her back, not covered by any kerchief.

At the end of the hall a hatch has been opened, and through it servants are handing out a breakfast of bread and beer. Breakfast is not a serious meal; no one sits down for it or spends more than a few minutes eating it. But everyone feels better after a little snack. Robert and William fetch breakfast for their mother and sister, a small loaf of fine wheaten bread and a horn of French wine. The boys fetch as much for themselves, but the butler watches carefully to make sure that lesser men do not get better food than they deserve. There are many different kinds of bread, from fine white wheat to coarse rye. Only the family drink wine every day, but for soldiers and servants there are many different grades of ale. No one has a hot or teetotal drink; there is no tea nearer than China. On a very cold morning mulled ale might be provided, but this is a mild July day.

There is a little talk, principally about the local news, or rather about the absence of it. News is nearly always news of war, but at present there seems to be no fighting nearer than Normandy. The gate of the bailey may stay open until sundown; if a few sentries keep watch, there is no need for further precautions.

An hour after sunrise everyone separates to begin the work of the day. The lady Gunhild carries off Matilda to the bower, where they will sit over their embroidery while a lady reads aloud from an improving book—a dull way to pass the morning, but today there is no interesting company in the castle. William and Robert join the crowd of able-bodied men who drift out to the stables.

In this castle there are twenty or thirty young men of military age. Since they all earn a living by fighting on horseback they are all interested in the stables. In official documents, which are always written in Latin, they are called *milites*, warriors. In French, the tongue they speak among themselves, they are *chevaliers*, horsemen; for a man who fights on foot hardly ranks as a warrior. But the local peasants call them knights, a rather derogatory term —it means a man who carries messages on horseback.

They are a kind of people scarcely known before the Conquest, and what the peasants have noticed about them is their horsiness, not their fighting ability.

In 1087 a knight need not be a gentleman by birth, or a man of means. He must be able to ride really well, and to fight mounted, but in social rank he may be anything between a common trooper and a great baron. He must possess his own armor and at least one good horse, probably two or three; so he must have had some money to begin with. But he can be hired for about the same wages as any other craftsman, and no one expects him to display polished manners.

But though a knight need not be a gentleman, all gentlemen are knights. The more important you are the more fighting you will have to do, and the only respectable way to fight is on horseback. At this moment the lord Richard is fighting as a knight in the King's army in Normandy, and he pays the forty other knights who ride behind him.

So the knights who have been left behind in Sussex will not be the best examples of their kind. Some, of course, are gentlemen of distinction: the seneschal and the constable and the steward, who manage the affairs of this English barony. To speak exactly, the seneschal is the supreme commander in the absence of the lord Richard, the constable manages the horses and stables, and the steward is in charge of finance. But they consider themselves more or less equal in rank and do one another's jobs as convenience dictates. No one will be surprised if the seneschal orders forage, the constable takes command of an outlying castle, or the steward leads a raiding party of horsemen.

At the moment there is peace in England, though not in Normandy, and all these knights are intent on morning stables. They troop out of the bailey together to see how their horses have come through the night.

In time of siege the horses would be tethered within the bailey, some actually on top of the *motte*. But during this peaceful July night they have been grazing near the castle. A warhorse must be given oats every day, but hay is too precious to be squandered when grass is available; in summer the horses ought to graze when it is safe. At dawn the grooms brought them into the stable to be cleaned and strapped. During daylight a knight may wish to ride his horse at short notice; the horse will stand ready in the shady stable, sheltered from sun and flies.

All the knights are French, and the grooms English. Neither can speak properly the language of the other But during the last twenty years most of the upper serv· ants have picked up a smattering of French words, and there are not a great many things you want to say to a groom in a stable. Perhaps some of the knights have learned a little English.

This difference of language is a difficulty that must be faced. We know that English was then even more different from French than it is now, that no Englishman, even by listening carefully, could make out what a Frenchman was saying. Yet armies of occupation manage with very few words, and in the England of 1087 the French were an army of occupation. King Edward the Confessor had appointed a good many Frenchmen to prominent positions, and the fishermen of Sussex must sometimes have wished to communicate with their fellows on the opposite shore. Even before 1066 there must have been a number of bilingual interpreters.

For a slightly later period we have a little direct evidence. When King Henry II was accosted by an English hermit in 1172, he turned at once to the nearest English-born knight to interpret for him. Sir Philip de Mark was of French descent, and presumably spoke French by the fireside; but the King took it for granted that he would have picked up some English from his nurse, and the King proved right. A famous anecdote about one of the murderers of Saint Thomas of Canterbury, an anecdote told to prove that his parents had been as wicked as he, indicates that his father and mother spoke English in the home circle; that story must go back to at least the 1140s. The best explanation is that in the later eleventh century, when men only a few miles away might speak a very different dialect, the English were good at coping with foreign languages. Of course, every clerk of the Western Church could speak and write fluently in Latin.

It seems safe to assume that the children of the lord Richard, born in England and brought up among English servants, would be able to speak an inaccurate and ungrammatical English. It is significant that about this time English, now seldom written by the educated, begins to lose its elaborate grammar.

All the knights look over their horses carefully, and see

that the grooms clean them properly. They talk learnedly among themselves about the remarkable forms of treatment recommended for sick horses. Even at the beginning of the twentieth century, stable lore was a strange mixture of superstition, rule of thumb, and mistaken theory; in the eleventh century, when no one knew of the circulation of the blood or of germs as a cause of infection, it must have been even more strange. But a horse is the most valuable possession of many knights, and in any case a fascinating subject of discussion. Knights could talk happily about horses for hours and hours.

Robert has been cleaning his own horse with a wisp of hay, under the eye of an elderly groom. A knight expects someone else to look after his horse for him; but in an emergency he must be able to do it himself, and he must learn in youth. If Robert were to shirk his task the groom might report him to the constable, who would beat him. But there is no danger of this, for Robert is fond of horses.

His next task is less pleasant, his riding lesson. First, someone puts over his head a heavy leather shirt which comes well down to his calves. A genuine coat of mail would be furnished with overlapping metal rings on the outside, but it is this metal covering which makes mail so expensive. There is no need to make genuine mail for a boy who will soon grow out of it.

Yet he must get used to riding inside the cumbrous garment. For the same reason, he rams on his head a stout leather helmet, and puts long sharp spurs on his heels. In the meantime his horse has been saddled and bridled. His next duty is to swing gracefully into the saddle.

The stirrup hangs low to make him ride with a straight leg. He gets his foot into it easily enough; but then he must give a really vigorous jump to clear the high guardboard at the back of the saddle. In front there is another wooden guard, equally high. Together they protect a rider low down, where the skirts of his mail divide to cover his thighs.

No one held his horse's head as he mounted; in fact a knight gave the beast a sly prod to make it move forward at the most awkward moment. A knight may have to mount a plunging horse in battle. A boy cannot practice serious fighting, but he must be capable of controlling any horse under any conditions. Robert picks up the reins carefully, for the horse might come over backwards if he pulled hard on the savage bit fixed high in its mouth.

The horse is now eager to get out of the bailey, but Robert must keep it dancing until he is properly armed. Hanging from the saddle, behind his left leg, is a light dummy shield. A genuine shield of leather on a wooden frame, big enough to cover a knight from neck to ankle, would be too heavy for him. But he must get used to riding with something big and awkward on his bridle arm.

The shield is about the right size, even though lighter than the real thing. He slips the strap over his right shoulder to take most of the weight, and puts his left forearm through the grips. Now a groom hands him a blunt lance and thus his right hand is too occupied to help with the reins. He must manage the reins with the fingers of his

left hand only. At last he is ready to ride out.

He is very firm in his saddle. The guardboards, the stirrups, the heavy clothing all anchor him so that he cannot be unseated by a sudden buck. But guiding his horse is another matter, and that is what he must practice today. A knight must be able to get his horse over any sort of country, and when he is using his sword he must put the beast into exactly the position he wants.

Knights rode where no later soldier would dream of bringing a horse. In the winter of 1070, King William led them over the Westmorland Fells, where nowadays the local farmers hunt foxes on foot. The knights of the First Crusade rode their horses over mountains which would seem to us impassable for mules. Before the Conquest, when some of Edward the Confessor's Norman guests were attacked by the men of Dover, they mounted their horses to fight in the barricaded streets of a crowded town. Robert must learn to take his horse wherever a man can climb without using his hands.

The management of the lance is not quite so important. Recently the method of using it has changed. At Hastings some knights charged with their lances brandished over their heads, to stab with them as though they were assagais. Robert, like most of his generation, tucks his lance under his right arm with the point projecting in front of his horse's left ear. He wants to gallop into his enemy, while at the same time presenting his own shielded left side. That will almost certainly break the lance, which will be of little use to him anyway after his horse has pulled up. But fighting with a sword is very much the same on horseback or on foot. He may practice that without his horse, provided he remembers that his left arm will always be busy with the shield, and that if he drops his sword he will be unable to pick it up again.

With an elderly knight as tutor Robert fords a stream at various awkward places where the horse does not want to cross. He scrambles up and down some steep slopes and gallops through patches of gorse to make the horse watch where it puts its feet. He does not jump any fences, because he will never meet a fence on campaign. No one shuts cattle behind a fence, because it is cheaper to hire a lad to herd them in the open. Sometimes you may see a thick thorn hedge round an isolated house, but it would be foolish to ride at it. The hedge was grown for defense and is certainly unjumpable.

Only after Robert has practiced cross-country riding for an hour or two is he allowed a few gallops at a target, lance in rest. But by this time his horse is tired, and he manages quite well. His horse has kept on its feet all morning, which is a good thing; for the rider is so fixed in the saddle that he is unlikely to fall clear.

The riding lesson ends before midday. Robert must make sure that his horse is properly rubbed down and fed, but he need not do it himself so long as he sees it done. Then he has a good wash at the trough, and puts over his tunic a smart supertunic. This is a garment of almost exactly the same shape, but a little shorter in the skirt so that it can be seen to be the upper of two.

Its neck and hem are decorated with bands of embroidery, and it is more evenly dyed than the everyday tunic. When he has put on clean shoes and combed his hair he is ready for dinner.

After riding for only an hour, William went off reluctantly to the chancery, the rather grand name for the well-lighted cabin in the bailey where the half-dozen clerks do their writing. There he has spent the rest of the morning at his lessons, supervised by one of the clerks, though he is more of a nuisance to busy men than an industrious pupil. His future is still undecided, except that when he grows up he will certainly be a knight. He will inherit none of the ancestral lands in Normandy. It is already settled custom that what has come by inheritance must go to the eldest son, so that the family may remain great and famous. But the lord Richard may do what he wills with his English land, which he has gained for himself. He may divide it; or he may leave the whole to his younger son, so that when England and Normandy are under different rulers there will be no divided loyalties. It is already known that King William intends that his second son and namesake shall be King of England after him, but the ancestral duchy of Normandy must go to his eldest son, in spite of the fact that Robert has made war on his father. Whatever happens, young William fitzRichard will have a few manors in England. That vague word "manor," applied to so many things of greatly differing value, means in the first place a source of income which will enable its possessor to live without manual labor.

William has been learning to ride, seriously and strenuously, for the last year. It is something a boy must learn as he grows. The normal theory is that a boy should begin riding about the age of seven, and that after the age of fourteen he will not improve. There is something to be said for the theory, and anyway, the men of the Middle Ages liked to divide human life into stages of seven years.

But someone in William's station in life ought to be able to read, and that is more difficult than riding.

Practically everything that is written, is written in Latin, a language he does not understand very well. The words sound like those of his native French, but their order in the sentence and their terminations are strange to him. He hears a lot of Latin spoken round him, in church and in the discussions of the clerks. He will never aspire to write Latin, so the grammar does not greatly matter. But when he is a grown man he will have to put his seal to legal documents; he ought to be able to read for himself any document he seals.

Another great difficulty is the many forms of handwriting. This is not because every scholar writes his own individual hand; at that time no one used handwriting, even an individual signature, to test the genuineness of a document. But every center of learning taught its own form of writing, so that anything written at Canterbury would be unlike anything written at Rouen. An added complication is that English uses a few letters unknown to the Latin alphabet, so that an Englishman might put one in by mistake when writing Latin. One of these let-

ters has slipped in among the Latin captions of the
Bayeux Tapestry.

If a writer is being deliberately ornamental it will be
almost impossible to read his work. But elaborate orna-
ment is usually reserved for well-known passages from
the Gospels or the Canon of the Mass, where a reader
needs only a few familiar letters to jog his memory. Anyway, beautifully painted books will not come into the
grubby hands of an eight-year-old.

What William has been trying to read is some of the
most difficult writing of his day: the records of a manor
court. These are written in haste, with a mass of contrac-
tions which make them almost like shorthand. If anything happens at the manor court which ought to be
preserved for posterity, the clerk will keep these records. If
they are not worth keeping, the parchment on which
they are written will be sponged until all the ink has been
removed. Then it may be used again, for parchment is
expensive.

Even though they live in a time of rapid change, these
people are always trying to bind generations yet unborn.
They cannot imagine that the details of daily life will ever
alter. King William has stepped into the shoes of the late
King Edward, and the lord Richard has stepped into the
shoes of a number of English landowners. But surely
these manors have always been here, with the same
boundaries and the same population, owing the same
rents and services to their lords? If we give an acre to the
parson of the parish, or fix the number of pigs which

may root for acorns in a particular wood, we must take great care to leave a permanent record for our descendants. They will be holding the same manors, and enjoying much the same income, in a thousand years' time.

This morning William recognized a number of words on his bit of parchment, partly because they were words you would expect to find in a note of that kind. He has done well, and his master did not beat him. For any slight fault the teacher beats his pupil with a stout stick across the shoulders; and William, who is very conscious of the honor and dignity of a fitzRichard, accepts the beatings without complaint.

The fitzRichards are tremendously proud of their noble ancestry, for all that it is less than two hundred years old. Rollo and his Vikings settled on the lower Seine in the year 911. The lord Richard can trace his descent from a reformed pirate who died about 945. Very quickly the whole family became thoroughly French, in language, in manners, and above all in their Christianity. When the young Duke William who is now King of England fought at Val-ès-Dunes to enforce his power over rebellious Normans, Richard's father was among his supporters. A poem was composed about that battle, to show how wicked were those rebels. One proof of their wickedness was that a rebel leader charged with the war-cry "Thor help me!" But even this pagan prayer was uttered in French.

Every Norman family changed all its manners and customs quite recently, and no family can be traced very far back. Yet they are all stiff with family pride. If a girl wants to marry some social inferior her brothers may very likely kill her to preserve the family honor. These new arrivals feel a tremendous class-consciousness.

A number of English families, on the other hand, can trace their ancestry back without doubt to the year 600, long before there were any Vikings, and by poems and legends back to Woden and so to Noah (as can Queen Elizabeth II at the present day). King Edward the Confessor belonged to the most ancient dynasty in Europe, ruling over an intensely aristocratic society. Yet in Norman eyes all English are much of a muchness. A wise man has said that "nobility is but ancient riches." In the eleventh century the riches need not be very ancient.

Now the horn is blown to announce that dinner is served, and all the inhabitants of the castle troop into the hall.

The hall is a long gabled building, profusely decorated. The ends of the roofbeams inside are carved into fantastic faces. The paneled walls are stained in a vivid pattern of red and green. On either side runs a line of square unglazed windows, though those on the windward wall have been closed by wooden shutters, so that light and air enter only from the lee side. But the vivid paint is dimmed by smoke, for a great fire smolders on a square hearthstone set in the wooden floor and there is no chimney. Holes in the roof above the hearth would carry away the smoke if there were no drafts, but with so many open windows there are always drafts blowing. Trestle tables are set down the length of this hall, where the lesser knights dine. At the sides, farther from the fire, are other tables for the servants. At the far end, on a low dias, is a short table where the family dines in state. They all sit side by side, facing down the hall, with the lady Gunhild in the middle. Any important guests would also be seated at the high table, but today there are none.

Besides Gunhild and her children a few important gentlemen and their ladies sit at this table, including the seneschal, and the steward, and the constable. The butler, who is nearly as grand as the other chief officers, will join them as soon as the meal has started. But since he is in charge of all the drink in the castle, whether wine or beer, he acts at the beginning as a kind of headwaiter, standing by in a long gown to see that everyone is served properly.

On the high table there is a linen cloth, and individual drinking horns. These are genuine horns, of cows or of wild bulls from the German forests, with little legs of silver gilt added so that they will stand on the table. Everyone brings his own knife, and his own spoon of horn or wood or silver. Forks are not used. There are no individual plates; instead they use flat loaves of white bread called manchets. You may finish by eating your manchet after it has sopped up the gravy, or you may leave it to be given to the beggers at the castle gate. By the end of the meal the tablecloth must have been in a mess, but that would be a sign of grandeur. In a baron's castle there should be plenty of maids to wash dirty tablecloths.

The lesser tables are of scrubbed boards, without covering. Again everyone brings his own knife and spoon. Most of the lesser men and women drink from plain cow's horns, which must be held in the hand until they are put down empty. They have no manchets, for wheaten bread is a luxury. A few fussy people bring platters of beechwood, but for most the clean boards are good enough to eat off.

They dine almost entirely on roast meat, beef or pork or mutton, and, if the fowlers have been lucky, quantities of small birds, also roasted whole and stuck on long spits. The food is handed round by servants; it is not yet the custom for young squires to wait at table. These servants are, of course, English. But they have picked up a few words of French, notably the names for the main foods.

At the high table there is wine in moderation; not too much, for it has to be imported from France. Normans hold it to be bad manners to get drunk in public in the middle of the day, though the English consider this to be a queer foreign whimsy. Also, the wine is rather nasty. It is served from leather bottles, so that at best it tastes of leather. The bottle stoppers are made of pitch, which tastes even worse, so that no one wants the first cup from a new bottle. Without airtight corks wine does not keep well, so there can be no fussing over vintages. It is conventional charity to give away your old wine to the poor; to give away new wine would be extravagantly saintly.

At the lesser tables they drink ale, which is brewed almost daily in many different strengths. Very small beer is a suitable drink for babies; strong ale is very strong indeed. But because hops are as yet unknown, none of it will keep for more than a few days before going sour.

It is about midday. Everyone has been busy since sunrise, and no one ate much of a breakfast. Dinner is a very solid meal indeed. For a good many of the lower orders there will be nothing more to eat until dinner tomorrow. The steward shudders to think of the number of beasts which must be slaughtered daily, but it would be shameful to stint dinner in a baron's hall. At the end of the meal nuts and apples and honey are handed round the high table, but not to the lesser folk. No green vegetables have been eaten.

Norman cooking is supposed to be better than English. But if a whole roast sheep is to be consumed there is nothing much to be done with it except roast it. So near the coast salt is plentiful, though farther inland it may be hard to come by; mustard and pepper are unknown. This meal has been very simply cooked.

But on a great many days in the year, every Friday and all the weekdays of Lent and Advent, no Christian may eat flesh. On those days, here in Sussex, they eat excellent sea fish, and the Norman cook displays his skill in devising pleasant sauces. But sea fish cannot be carried far before it goes bad. Luckily salmon and other good fish abound in most of the rivers of England; or you might take a chance and eat tainted sea fish, which killed a good many eminent men at that period. On such days of abstinence even men of means might eat a good deal of bread, which they found not really so bad if it had first been soaked in wine.

At the high table ladies and gentlemen sit together, and so do the male and female servants in the body of the hall. This is a Norman innovation; the old English custom was to separate the sexes. But then in this new-fangled castle no one is allowed to get properly drunk at dinner. Neither is there any flirtation. Courteous love has not yet been invented, even in Aquitaine where it first arose; wives sit beside their husbands, who will be jealous and heavy-handed if a stranger talks too much.

At the high table, conversation is about the King's great inquiry into the rights and obligations of all the landholders of England, which is being copied even now into the great volumes of the Domesday Book. Last year the King's commissioners visited every manor in the country, and asked the most searching questions. At the time nobody knew exactly what the King was after, and even historians of the present day are not quite sure. As much as anything, the commissioners seemed anxious to know how much tax was due from which arable field, so that the right defaulter could be punished if the total fell short.

The whole idea of paying a tax in money is strange to free Norman barons. In Normandy they never did anything of the kind, and no other kingdom in Western Christendom has anything like the English system of taxation. But the system is not quite so unbearable as it sounded when first explained to them. In theory every hide of arable land should pay so many pennies in the pound of its annual value, at a rate fixed only at the King's discretion. But this tax has been levied for a very long time, longer than the Normans have been settled in Normandy.

How big is a hide? Normally, 120 acres. How big is an

acre? Normally, a day's work for a plow. The villagers remember how many hides there used to be in their ancestors' time, when the tax was first imposed. They disregard land which has been cleared since. But if land has gone out of cultivation, through devastation in war or by a natural fall in population, they never fail to point it out to the commission. All sorts of other factors come in. A piece of land was once held by a personal friend of some dead king, who let him off part of his tax; that right will continue forever. The net result is that the number of reputed hides paying tax bears very little relation to the area of land actually under plow. It is interesting to learn how much ought to be paid by each manor of the barony, but that will be no indication of the amount of the expected harvest.

It is not easy for a foreigner to understand English money in general. This tax is called a *geld*; though in fact it is paid in silver, for no gold is coined in England. English clerks, like the clerks of all Western Christendom, reckon their accounts in pounds, shillings, and pence, a legacy from the last days of the Roman Empire. But a silver coin that weighed a pound would be a clumsy thing to carry about. The only coin actually struck is a silver penny, one-twelfth of a shilling, 240 to the pound. In the Danish parts of England, the eastern Midlands and the North, they reckon in "hundreds of silver," not in pounds. The Danish idea of a hundred—for those pirates were once very lavish with their money—is what we should call 120; so that "a hundred of silver" equals ten shillings or half a pound. By the eleventh century this is not often written down, but it still survives in popular speech.

King William claims the sole right to coin English money, by inheritance from the old English kings. He employs a great many moneyers in every important commercial town, and though the dies are all supplied by his treasury some moneyers are more accurate than others. Once the pennies are in circulation wicked men clip bits off them, so that what looks like a sound silver penny may not be worth its face value. When pennies reach the treasury they are first weighed and then "blanched," melted to discover the proportion of genuine silver. Nearly always the payment is a few pennies short.

In France, where all these people came from, every great lord coins his own money. The best money is struck in Tours, and most people in France reckon in money of Touraine; but counts and dukes and bishops issue many odd lumps of metal, so that large sums can be paid only by weight. The fine coinage of England, the best until you reach Byzantium far off to the east, is a great convenience. But still you are never quite sure how much the King will demand from you.

This worries the seneschal. He suggests that they should have taken advantage of the visit of the Domesday commissioners to fix a maximum sum that can be demanded from the barony in any one year. And what about knight service? It has been agreed that the lord Richard owes forty knights to the King. In fact he employs sixty-five, so that ought to be easy. But must all forty serve the King whenever he asks for them, 365 days in the year if necessary? And the lord Richard himself? Will he never have by right any time for his own private affairs?

The lady Gunhild says that these questions need not be answered in writing, to bind all succeeding barons until the end of time. They will answer themselves, by ordinary give and take. All Normans must stick together—and King William is a Norman—or they will not long continue to rule the land of England. The King prefers money to personal service; then he can hire mercenaries, who are more easily controlled than barons. But if he asks too much from his barons, they can quite easily turn him off the throne and set up someone else in his stead. The King and his barons are in this enterprise together, and neither side dares quarrel with the other.

The seneschal complains that having so many idle knights hanging about the castle is a great nuisance. They are noisy and quarrelsome, they drink too much, and they bully the servants. It would be better for discipline if they were given land of their own and told to live on it until their services were required. Sensible religious houses have been dispersing their knights in this way, for the sake of peace and quiet.

It is a threadbare topic, and the lady Gunhild answers wearily. Idle knights are more of a bother to monks than to laymen. She likes to see plenty of knights about the castle, as an example to her sons who will be knights when they are older. If these men were given land of their own they might not come readily when they are needed. Many of them have got it into their heads that forty days of castleguard each year is the limit of their unpaid duty in time of peace. Above all, to give land to all the knights would be very expensive. At any given moment many of them would be too old or too young or too sick to come to the muster. They would have to send a substitute, and at the same time support themselves. So that enough land to endow a knight would have to be worth much more than will actually pay a knight.

Then the seneschal adds that he gathers from what the Domesday commissioners said to him that the King would like to see more knights settled on their own land. Gloomily the lady Gunhild agrees that they will have to do as the King wishes. There is a great deal of law in England, rather more than suits a free and independent Norman baron; but that law does not cover barons, a new class of men that did not exist in the days of King Edward. King William invents baronial law as he goes along, pushing the rights of the crown as far as he dares. If he were to take a dislike to the fitzRichards, the house would not endure for long. After next harvest they will begin to distribute their land into knights' fees, which will, of course, descend from father to son like all other landed property.

As he listens to this conversation Robert feels rather grand. One day he will be a baron in succession to his father; it is nice to know that the kingdom will stand only so long as the barons support it. On the other hand, the barons do in fact support it, and he must take care not to revolt while his fellows are loyal. He is beginning to see that whatever may be the legal position, England is ruled by the public opinion of its great landholders. In those days that was not true of France or of any other Christian kingdom; it was the first beginning of the English Constitution.

When the lady Gunhild gives the signal to rise, they have sat over dinner for barely an hour. Everyone has shoveled in a great deal of food very fast, for there are as yet no rules about table manners except the elementary rule that you must keep yourself and your clothes clean. The English servants, and a few English wayfarers who have been given hospitality at the lesser tables, consider this an absurdly short time to spend over the main meal of the day, but they are resigned to it as another queer Norman custom. The butler sees that the tables are taken off their trestles and stacked with the benches alongside the walls, so that no one may loiter in idleness with his drinking horn.

It is still early afternoon, but the gentry consider they have done a day's work and may amuse themselves until sunset. The knights are at a loose end. Few of them have enough horses to go riding again as they did in the morning, and anyway there is nowhere amusing to visit. If they go to the buttery and clamor for more wine it will be difficult for the English servants to deny them, but the lady Gunhild will be very angry. If they sit down in the sun and gamble, at checkers or at dice, that will lead to quarrels, and they are all hot-tempered men, with swords handy. Some of them can read, but with such an effort that they get no pleasure from it; and in the castle there are no books intended for recreation. What to do with knights when they are not busy fighting is an unsolved problem.

Some knights are married, and they stroll off into the woods with their wives. On a fine summer afternoon a married couple may enjoy a little privacy. At night they sleep in rows on the floor, and when the weather is bad in daytime, everyone shelters somewhere under a crowded roof. The people of the eleventh century did not like living in a perpetual crowd any more than we do; in winter all castle-dwellers longed for the coming of spring especially because it gave them an opportunity to get away from prying eyes.

The lady Gunhild passes the afternoon nodding over her embroidery in a snug private chamber behind the bower. In her youth, before the fitzRichards became so grand, she rode on many campaigns with her lord; long journeys in wet clothes have given her perpetual rheumatism. Now that she is old and successful enough to sit at home in her fine castle, she never wants to do anything else.

The three children go hunting, mounted on quiet ponies convenient to their size. The head huntsman is in charge of them, with a few knights as bodyguard and some kennelboys on foot to look after the dogs. One should say dogs rather than hounds, for this is nothing like a pack. The children are out to catch any small animals, mainly for the pot. The King will not allow his subjects to hunt deer, even in their own woods.

This is a tyrannous and unpopular measure, but King William has the law on his side. At least since the days of

King Canute all the deer in England have belonged to the King. That is not the law in France, where the King has little power; but the King of France is just strong enough to prevent the Duke of Normandy from claiming to own all the deer in his duchy. As a result the lord of any French forest may hunt deer in it.

In the early days of the Conquest most Normans did not suppose that the niggling, bothersome English game laws could apply to *them*. But the King has made the point very clear. He has made a wooded district of Hampshire into a new royal forest, though that meant the desecration of two or three parish churches. Everyone prophesies darkly that such unchristian preference for beasts over men will one day bring bad luck to the house of Rollo; the New Forest will be an unchancy place for kings. But in the meantime it would be foolish to annoy the King by hunting his deer.

There are, however, other creatures in the woods worth eating. The best fun would be to find a hare, but it would probably run over standing crops and July is a bad month for riding through them. Of course, the children have a right to ride over the fields of their father's peasants, but at this time of year even the head huntsman would consider it silly and wasteful, as impoverishing the whole barony. So the greyhounds, coupled and led by men on foot, are out chiefly for air and exercise.

There are rabbits in plenty, skipping among the roots of the oak trees. They never run far, so you can't gallop after them on a horse; but by blocking some burrows with nets and then sending down little terriers to flush the rabbits, you may get some excitement and fill the larder. In a few weeks, after the harvest has been reaped, the children may ride in line over the stubble to drive partridges into nets spread to catch them. But partridges are birds of the cultivated fields, and it would be wrong to go after them in July.

As their ponies wade through the high bracken, Matilda puts up a cock pheasant. Such rare creatures are highly valued. Everyone halts, still and silent, to mark where it settles in a high tree. Then little William slips off his pony and creeps forward with a stonebow. This is a short, stiff bow with a small pouch in the middle of the string. It shoots pebbles, or in this case bullets of baked clay, which kill birds without knocking them to pieces as an arrow would.

William is proud of his skill with the stonebow. He creeps close to the sitting pheasant and kills it with a direct hit from his clay bullet. Here is a trophy to remember, and a dish to test the skill of the cook. For tomorrow's dinner the chief cook will remove the skin and feathers in one piece, roast the bird, and then slip the skin on again so that it appears at the table in all its glory. It will also be neither hot nor cold, and so freshly killed that it would seem tough to our taste; but at that time nobody bothered about these disadvantages. The kitchen was so far from the hall, for fear of fire, that all dishes arrived at the table lukewarm; and the meat, unless it had been salted, was always so freshly killed that it must be tough.

Throughout the Middle Ages pheasants were rare and

treasured luxuries. They are not native to England. The Romans brought them from the Black Sea, and often the English winter is too cold for them. The pheasant hen is a very incompetent mother, and in the eleventh century no one feeds the young chicks and protects them from vermin, so that few of them survive until they are big enough to fly. You will note, also, that there is no close season for any beast or bird. If the weather is good enough to go out riding, you chase anything that gets up and runs away—except, of course, the King's deer. All birds are shot sitting, unless you drive them into nets; with no missile more accurate than arrow or clay bullet, it would be a waste of time to shoot flying. Hunting is still very much a search for food; it has not yet become an elaborate sport, bound by rules.

When the children are grown up they may be invited to hunt deer with the King, which is more of a sport than the scavenging they are doing today. Hunting deer is chiefly a test of horsemanship, like most other knightly exercises. Beaters on foot rouse the deer, unless some skilled forester has lain out all night to keep an eye on where a great stag is harboring. In the morning hounds are laid on, so that the stag cannot hide again in some thick patch of undergrowth, and the mounted hunters set themselves to ride it down. It is a point of honor to ride wherever the stag has gone, and according to the few surviving pictures of those times the favorite place to ride is the middle of the pack. All the time he crashed through the bushes the foremost hunter blew his horn to tell his companions where the hunt was going. When he got close enough to his quarry he shot it down with an arrow, at full gallop.

Some people were very much better at this kind of cross-country gallop than others; if they happened to be great men, you can still read how they often lost all their fellow huntsmen and in the end got lost themselves. It seems strange that these noblemen, who constantly used the bow in hunting, never shot an arrow in war; but to use the bow called for an unencumbered left arm, and no horseman would go into battle without a heavy triangular shield.

While the children potter about in the woods, they are enjoying one of the happiest afternoons they can remember. Within the broad limits allowed by the chief huntsman they are free to amuse themselves as they wish. That is a rare treat.

In the eleventh century there was little sympathy for childhood. Babies were known to be helpless, and precious; but as soon as a human being had attained the age of reason, which most theologians fixed at seven years, he or she was expected to behave like a little adult. Decorum was demanded in public, and obedience all day long. Boys must put up with rough treatment, and girls behave like dignified ladies.

As the sun sinks, the children ride home. They can talk among themselves of the future arranged for them. Robert, of course, will be heir to the barony, and he knows more or less what he must do. He will be a leading member of the company of Norman knights who have conquered all the land of England. Fighting will be his chief occupation, and that means more than charging gallantly when the time comes. On any battlefield he will command a considerable squadron of knights; at the moment his father leads forty knights in Normandy, and for a really decisive battle, if the future of the barony were at stake, he could muster about seventy in all. It is very likely that one day Robert will be the most important baron with the army; then he will be expected to give the order to charge.

They have all been brought up on the story of Hastings, the greatest battle that their father ever saw. They have heard all about the initial repulse, and how the knights returned to the charge; of William riding bareheaded down the line to prove that the rumor of his death was false; of the two feigned flights; of Harold's death and the final collapse of the English shield wall. It was the most important battle of the century, the most stubbornly fought and the most cleverly contested. The enemy remained immovable throughout, or at least that was what Harold intended, but the Norman leader was the mighty William, the greatest soldier and the most powerful ruler of his age. *He* could bring back his knights to the charge after they had flinched, *he* could persuade them to pretend to be beaten and to come back fighting. Robert does not suppose that his men will ever follow him like that.

Especially against a mounted foe, Robert's men will have one good charge in them. If they win they will immediately pursue for so long as their horses can gallop. If they think they are being worsted they will run away very suddenly, and run for miles in the hope of getting clear of pursuit. Their one charge must be delivered at exactly the right moment.

When he is old enough to fight, in about five years, Robert will be unable to delegate the responsibility of command. By then his father will be growing a bit old for active service, and will be glad to see his heir lead the knights of the barony. If Robert is the knight of highest birth present, everyone will look to him for orders even if he has never fought before. He may be able to consult quietly with some trusted veteran, but the orders will have to issue from his own mouth. Many years later the untried King Edward II had to command the army of England against the veteran Robert Bruce, King of Scotland, though he had plenty of veteran knights serving under him, and he duly led it to defeat at Bannockburn. In the Middle Ages the chain of command followed strictly the table of precedence.

Robert is haunted by the prospect of his first battlefield, when he will have to begin his military service at the top. If his first charge succeeds, he will quickly make a name for himself; if it fails, he will be expected to be the last knight to flee. It will all be a terrible gamble.

When he succeeds to the barony he will face another onerous duty, though his father will fulfill it as long as he lives, even after he is long past fighting. He will have to advise the King in council. Every vassal must advise his lord whenever called upon; he may not excuse himself for fear of making personal enemies, and he must give his advice in public if that is how his lord wants to hear it.

When he succeeds his father, the King of England will be his lord, whoever may be King of England when that distant day arrives. One of the meanings of that elastic term "baron" is a landholder who obeys no lord except the King. There was a time when every free warrior was called "baron," and the term embedded in ancient laws sometimes causes confusion. "Baron" is also used loosely to denote any considerable landholder, even if his lord is a duke or a count; but in its most accurate sense it means someone like the lord Richard, and eventually Robert fitzRichard will succeed to all his rights and duties.

Robert will have to do homage for his barony to the King, placing his hands between the King's hands and swearing to serve him faithfully. Anyone may do homage to the King without loss of dignity; but if Robert is called on to be the man of some other baron, as a condition of holding land from him, he will do his best to wriggle out of the obligation—provided, of course, that he may keep the land.

There never was a feudal *system*, in England or in any other Western country, and in the eleventh century the feudal way of doing things was very far from systematic. Three elements were mixed up in it: personal honor, money, and land. From the earliest times free German warriors had sworn loyalty to a chosen lord; and both the Normans and the Franks of France who lived beside them had been in origin free German warriors. Those early comrades who took oath to a chosen lord expected the lord to supply them with food, lodging, clothes, and

arms for as long as they should live; in return they owed him unlimited military service against any foe, to the point where they ought not to survive him if he were killed in battle. Some of that feeling would still bind Robert, especially if the King in person had led him into battle. For example, he would probably feel that honor compelled him to throw away his own life if that was the only way for the King to get away from a lost field.

But nowadays he need not always follow the King to battle. The theory has grown up that he is bound only to defend the King's dominions, England and Normandy. If he were summoned to invade Wales or Scotland he might refuse, provided enough of the other barons would stand by him. His father refused to invade England as a matter of feudal duty, though after he had been promised a share in the profits he came willingly as a volunteer. Nowadays the King does not feed and lodge his barons in his own hall. Instead he gives them land. So they must have some time to themselves, to look after their estates. Even when they follow him willingly to war, they begin to grumble if the campaign goes on too long. There is no fixed rule, but most people agree that a knight ought to serve his lord, without pay, for forty days in time of peace. That will be to garrison his castles, of course. Forty days in the year? Or forty days at a stretch, with a decent break before garrison duty comes round again? That has not yet been decided.

The boring drudgery of sentry-go need not be performed in person. Any baron may hire another knight to do it for him; but the baron, not the King, will pay the deputy. In the same way any baron will fight for the King, at the head of all his knights, for at least forty days at his own expense. But if the campaign drags on he will begin to expect pay sometime in the seventh week. If no pay is forthcoming he will not normally go home; that would be the dishonorable felony of deserting his lord in the field. But he will be a slack and unwilling warrior.

Again, all this may be done by deputy if the baron is too old or too young for active service, or if she happens to be a lady. As a rule a Norman lady ranked as heiress after her brothers but before her uncles and cousins, though it was a rule with many exceptions.

One of the things the Domesday Book was drawn up to settle was how many knights were due from each piece of land. That is now on record, but like every other administrative measure of the eleventh century it is subject to adjustment. Some barons like fighting, and hope to win fame as warriors; others are more interested in managing their land. First of all the King wants good knights, well armed and well mounted; among good knights he prefers those who look to him for their daily pay, as more likely to obey his orders. Very often a baron will please the King better by paying generously for mercenaries than by serving in person with his own knights.

The King can keep his throne only so long as most of his barons are loyal to him. But barons also dread rebellion, since their main title to their land is that the King gave it to them. So neither King nor baronage make a practice of standing on the letter of their rights.

Every baron admits that the King ought to get some

profit from his kingdom. When the lord Richard dies his barony will, in strict legal theory, revert to the King, though it would be very shocking if the King were to grant it to anyone except Robert, the legal heir. Yet Robert ought to pay a "relief" for it, the equivalent of an inheritance tax. He would be willing to pay about a years' income, which is generally admitted to be fair. If the King asks for much more Robert will turn sulky, and may think of rebellion; if the King likes him personally, he may ask for less. But this is unlikely, for reliefs are the most important part of the King's cash revenue, and the King is always hard pressed for money.

The King's next most important right, universally admitted by his barons, is to be guardian of his vassal's widow and infant children. If the lord Richard were to drop dead tomorrow, the King would administer the barony until Robert came of age. Probably he would put in a royal official to do it, but he might order the lady Gunhild to marry some friend of his. Then Gunhild's second husband would be baron until Robert was old enough to succeed. The orphaned Matilda would be married to the highest bidder, provided he were of equal social rank, though the bid would not be very high since two healthy brothers stand between her and the barony. Young William would be reared at the King's expense until he was old enough to go out into the world, then turned adrift with horse and arms or hired as a royal mercenary. The other barons would be sorry for the bad fortune which had come to the fitzRichards, but because they claim the same right over their own knightly tenants they would have to stand by the King. Only if Gunhild or Matilda were "disparaged" by being married to some man of low birth would there be general discontent. That was something barons would not stand, one of the chief reasons why they turned against King John in the thirteenth century.

You see that there is not much system in this feudalism. It is very like bargaining over wages between some great trades union and an industry. The King is more powerful than any baron; all the barons together are more powerful than the King. But they are in the same boat, as rulers of a conquered and discontented country, so they must pull together.

William is too young to think seriously of the future. He takes it for granted that when he has grown up someone will give him horse and arms and send him out to seek his fortune. If his father is still alive there will probably be a great feast in the castle. But a knight is any man who knows how to fight on horseback, not yet a man vowed to any chivalrous ideal; there will be no solemn quasi-religious ceremony.

He may seek his fortune in England. It would be easiest to enlist with the King or to take wages from his brother. But that would be dull. In many parts of Christendom, Norman knights are welcome. All Italy south of Rome is ruled by the sons of Tancred of Hauteville, a simple Norman knight of no particular distinction. One of them would be glad to hire another genuine Norman lance. In Spain the Kings of Navarre, Aragon, and Castile are pushing back the infidel Moors, and they welcome all recruits. If he does not mind the climate, there is Scotland, whose King is turning the whole country upside down. First he married an English princess, and made his Celtic court adopt English ways. Now he prefers Norman manners, and hires Norman knights to teach his warriors how to fight on horseback. William is quite sure that one day he will fight for his bread and end up as a great lord. Where he will fight can be settled later.

Matilda's future is coming very near, and she can do nothing to influence it. Next year, or the year after, she will be betrothed, and married soon after her thirteenth birthday. Her parents are now looking for a suitable husband, and they will not consult her until the man has been chosen. If she then takes a strong dislike to him her parents, kindly people, will try again. But she must not be too difficult to please. She will have to marry some Norman gentleman whose friendship will be useful to the house of fitzRichard, and there are not a great number to choose from.

If she hated the thought of marriage she might become a nun instead. But she feels no vocation for the religious life, and for a woman it has no secular advantages. Most nunneries are poor and not very solvent foundations. In the old days, some convents were famous; in England especially they used to be full of kings' daughters. But nowadays zeal has slackened and nuns are not very much esteemed. In the days of St. Boniface there were abbesses in England famous for their learning; now the nuns of England produce excellent embroidery.

So marriage it must be, and on the whole there might

be worse. Her husband will not be the man of her choice, but she will be his partner. When he is away from home she will command his castle, as the lady Gunhild now commands here. Of course, if they should quarrel she may expect a bad time. Public opinion would not be shocked if he beat her, or locked her up in a tower. But unless she is obviously in the wrong her brothers will take offense. In Normandy they might wage war on him. Could they wage a private war in England? That is forbidden by the old law of England, and no one would dare to try it while King William reigns. But the law was made for man, not man for the law; later kings may not wish to interfere between angry brothers-in-law. At any rate, her future husband will be careful not to annoy the fitzRichards.

But it is nearly time for supper, and she has not yet put on her supertunic. When the horn sounds again, about dusk, the hall fills as the family take their places at the high table. They are not offered the solid roasts of dinner. This is a lighter meal, of cold meat and reheated stews and pastry. But drink is more plentiful, since this is the end of the day.

As more drink is passed round, a *jongleur* stands up to entertain the company. A *jongleur* is a juggler, but this man is not very clever at catching colored balls. However, he knows a new version of the exploits of William of Orange, one of the legendary heroes who served Charlemagne. He has learned it by heart, and intends to travel through England for a year, singing it in various castles. If he had composed his own song he would be a *trouvère*, of a much higher social class, worthy to sit at the high table. But all Normans remember that a juggler named Ironbiter was the first Norman to kill an Englishman at Hastings as he juggled with his sword. In England jugglers are treated with respect.

When he has finished it is quite dark outside. Servants clear away the trestle tables and fill the hall with trestle beds. Here the senior knights and their wives will sleep, cozy but crowded, for in all this large company only the lady Gunhild has a private bedroom.

When they go to bed they are all sober, which is one of the most striking changes in manners since 1066.

II · A SOCMAN
AND HIS FAMILY

The Domesday commissioners recorded of Godric that in Berkshire he held three hides of land, and might go with them where he would. That conveys rather a charming picture of Godric picking up three hides—about 360 acres—and carrying them off on his back to, say, Wiltshire, to avoid the floods of the Thames Valley. But even though the Domesday commissioners believed some remarkably tall stories told them by English villagers, they would not believe that. What they were saying in their legal shorthand is that Godric is not quite grand enough to hold a court of his own to keep order among his peasants, but that he may choose which court, among those held by his more powerful neighbors, should be responsible for law and order on his land. He is a socman, coming within the soc, or jurisdiction, of his chosen lord.

It was a valuable privilege, which did not long endure. After 1087 there is no record of a socman changing the lord to whom he owed allegiance when Domesday Book was compiled. Presumably such an upheaval would have caused more trouble than it was worth. But Godric himself has made a free choice, and he did not know at the time that it would bind his descendants for ever.

Godric can trace back his ancesters for many generations. One of them fought under King Alfred against the Viking forefathers of these Normans. Local peasants regard him as a nobleman, but the present ruling class think nothing of English pedigrees. He still has his land because he kept out of all the troubles of 1066. In those days his father was alive, a devoted adherent of King Edward. There was some doubt about whom King Edward had chosen as heir, but no doubt at all that it was not Earl Harold. Godric should have marched with the fyrd, the English militia, to Stamford Bridge, but his father advised him to plead sickness and stay at home; in the hurried march back from Yorkshire to Hastings so many fell out through exhaustion that no one noticed his absence from the final battle. Since then he has faithfully accepted King William as ruler of England.

The same July day of 1087 dawns over his hall. The hall is a solid building of timber and clay, about a hundred years old, more solid and weatherproof than any of the huts in the Norman bailey. Round it stand a number of flimsy cabins not built to last: barns, dairies, store-rooms, and a kitchen which is burned down on purpose at fairly frequent intervals when it becomes too sooty and smelly. The whole space of nearly an acre is enclosed by a strong hedge of thorn, with a single gate in it. This hedge is not a serious defense against armed men, though it might stop a knight who tried to gallop right up to the hall; but under old English law it had great importance. It used to define the limits of Godric's personal peace, so that any man who used a weapon within it must pay compensation to Godric as well as to the King. No one is quite sure whether that law still holds good under the new dynasty. Usually King William punishes peace-breakers with blinding and mutilation; he will not take money from them instead.

The inside of this hall is surprisingly comfortable. Down the middle runs a long hearth which in winter may be filled with burning logs, though in July only a small fire smolders in it. Of course, there is no chimney, but the roof is so high that the smoke gathers well above the floor. On either side of the fire trench are the living quarters. These are divided naturally into bays by the pillars supporting the roof. A few curtains can make any of these bays into a private sleeping chamber. At dawn all the inhabitants are getting dressed, and taking down their curtains as soon as they are fit to appear in public.

At the far end is a dais, and behind it a little cubbyhole where Godric and his wife, Godgifu, sleep well away from drafts. On both sides of the hall just below the dais are the bed-places of the chief men of the house and of the chief ladies. In one sleep Godgifu's two sons, Edward and Wulf, aged fourteen and ten; opposite sleeps her daughter, aged twelve. Lower down, nearer to the door at the far end, sleep less important men and married couples. They have a good deal more quiet, privacy, and space than the Normans in their warlike castle.

The boys put on thick woolen shirts, linen drawers, and woolen stockings ending below the knee. The stockings are kept in place by leg bandages like modern puttees, but these are not wound into an elegant crisscross pattern. That would be too grand for the boys' station in life. They wear leather shoes, fastened at the ankle with a buckle. Last of all they slip over their heads loose tunics of unbleached wool, with a plain leather girdle round the waist to support a wallet made of cowskin with the hair left on.

After they have washed face and hands rather sketchily at the trough in the yard, they use it as a mirror to comb their hair. This is worn as long as possible, down to the shoulders, and arranged very carefully with a parting in the middle. In the eleventh century everyone dresses in accordance with his station in life; a respectable English boy would have been as ashamed of too grand a costume as of wearing the clothes of a laborer. Well-combed clean hair is a mark that you do not work all day with your hands, and that it is long shows that you do not wear the helmet of a knight.

Their sister, Edith, has recently been promoted out of the short tunic and bare legs appropriate to a child of either sex. By the time she pulls aside the curtains of her bed-place she is almost entirely concealed by loose clothing, so covered that it is impossible to say whether she is fat or thin. Over a smock like a man's shirt, except that it comes down to her ankles, she has put on a long loose kirtle with wrist-length sleeves. Over that is a supertunic, just a little shorter in the skirt and with wide elbow-length sleeves. On top of all this a white veil is draped over her head and shoulders to conceal her hair and encircle her face. It is a costume in which it is impossible to take active exercise.

Godric wears a short tunic like his sons, and a cloak fastened at one shoulder with an enameled brooch. His drawers, stockings, and leg bandages are of the same kind, but on his feet he wears leather ankle-boots, very loose at the top and needing no fastening. His rank and dignity are shown chiefly by the adornment of his head. His hair, parted in the middle, hangs well down on his shoulders; his mustaches stick out so far that they can be seen from behind; his whiskers end in a long forked beard lying on his chest. On his head he wears, indoors and out, a high bonnet of embroidered cloth. His girdle is of plain leather and supports a plain leather wallet. Godgifu is dressed in the same manner as her daughter, though since she is growing stout the effect is even more cumbrous.

None of the men or boys carries any kind of weapon openly; they would consider it barbarous to go armed unless fully equipped for war. But everyone has on him a short eating-knife, carried inside the wallet; and we know, from surviving criminal records, that this could be used to kill a man in the course of a quarrel. In the Middle Ages, sticking a knife into your enemy was a very common English pastime.

A number of other people have slept in the hall, not all of them dependents of Godric. There are no hotels or lodging houses where you may hire a bed for the night, except in a few large towns; and most taverns only sell ale. On a journey you must ride, or walk if you cannot afford a horse, and for food and lodging seek hospitality from some house you approach in the evening. It must have been rather a trying business, calling for tact and good manners. Norman knights, on horseback, are the rulers; they must be accommodated anywhere, or they will know the reason why. But the native English are divided into many social classes, and each will expect to be treated as befits his rank. A man in Godric's position must offer hospitality to all comers, but not to all comers equally; he himself may sometimes have been puzzled or embarrassed.

Any kind of clerk, from a beneficed priest to a scribe in very minor orders, would carry a certificate from the bishop who had ordained him. He would be quite easy to please, though, of course, if it fitted in with his plans he would prefer to pass the night in a monastery or priory. Then there are a number of professional pilgrims, laymen who wander from one holy shrine to another. They also will carry some document to prove that they are genuine holy men, and it will be fairly easy to look after them; for they will expect to eat coarse food and sleep on hard beds, to increase the merit of their pilgrimage. Very often they bring interesting or at least amusing news from the last shrine they have visited, and they are always welcome.

Merchants are more difficult to place. The old English law honored merchants who ventured overseas, as it honored anyone connected with seafaring. But Normans despise those who make a living out of commerce, and the clergy in general suppose that if buying to sell again shows a profit there must be dishonesty at the root of it. A wealthy merchant, leading a train of pack ponies, wants chiefly safety for his goods. He may pass a night with Godric, for Godric's stockade is the strongest for some miles round. But he likes best to shelter within a walled town, or failing that, in a castle. He will not bother much about his entertainment, for he will pass most of the night fussing over his baggage. He will bring a great many men, as well as animals, and altogether put Godric to a good deal of expense. It would be shameful to present him with a bill in the morning; hospitality must always be free, which is why it is sometimes embarrassing to both parties. But a wealthy merchant can make a present to the lady of the house, or sell some luxury to his host at a cheap rate, to make sure that he will be welcome if he should want to come that way again.

The real puzzle to an honest householder are poor strangers with no documents to prove their identity. Since the land of a great baron may be scattered all over England, a poor freeman may have to travel from Yorkshire or Devon to bring suit at the main court of the barony in Sussex. A man who turns up at dusk, on foot, may be genuinely on his way to his lord's court, or he may be a rogue on the run. To turn him away would be shameful, but Godric may get into trouble with the law if he shelters him. Peddlers are even more of a nuisance. The packs on their backs prove that they have an honest means of earning a living, but it is widely suspected that most peddlers rob lonely housewives if they get the chance. For the sake of his own good name, Godric cannot turn away any man who comes to his house in daylight; after dark the dogs are loose and no stranger is admitted within the stockade. But one should always take a good look at poor travelers, and be ready to set the sheriff's men on their track if they prove to be wanted by the law.

Except when he is seeing that his peasants do their work properly, the law is Godric's main preoccupation. For most of today he will be in court. Only two strangers passed the night in his hall; they are both traveling peddlers, local men well known to him. The whole household stands round the fire, eating a light breakfast of porridge, bread, and ale; then the travelers set out on their journey.

Godric grumbles a bit about having to waste the day on public duties. Under this present king they come round much more frequently than in the past. The trouble is that the Norman sheriff makes everyone do all he is supposed to do. Godric owes suit to the manor court of his lord, which meets once a month. This means that he has to attend and take part in all the business of the court. He also owes suit to the hundred court, which meets every six weeks, and to the shire court, which meets three times in the year. In King Edward's time his father, who owed the same obligations, seldom bothered to turn up at any of these meetings unless a case was due to be heard which might concern him personally. Even in those days there was supposed to be a fine for absence without due cause, but nobody bothered about the letter of the law. Now these penalties are rigorously enforced.

Today he must attend the hundred court, the court of the "hundred," or subdivision, of the shire in which he lives. He has decided to bring young Edward with him so that the boy may begin to learn the business which will eventually become his responsibility. As he waits for the horses to be brought round to the door, Godric complains that such frequent sessions of the court manufacture work for the suitors, as those who have to attend are called. A hundred court ought not to be very important. Its chief work is to witness transfers of land between free men who hold of different lords, a pretty rare occurrence, and to apprehend petty criminals for subsequent trial before the shire court. Hardly anyone brings a civil action in the hundred court; most civil disputes are so petty that they can be settled within the manor, or so important that they go straight to the shire court.

But once the suitors have been assembled in one place someone will think of something they ought to decide. They may as well lay a charge against someone, and compel him to give sureties that he will answer the charge in

the shire court. Nearly everyone has put himself slightly wrong with the law, for the law is very complicated and men are very sinful. But no one would have bothered to lay a charge if they had not all been assembled in court with nothing better to do.

Godric reminds his son that a suitor in any court bears a great responsibility. He may offer to take oath on behalf of one of the parties; though unless he is quite sure that his man is in the right he would do well to keep out of it, or he may incur some of the spiritual guilt of perjury. Even if he refrains from lending his oath he certainly may not remain neutral. The verdict must be given by those suitors who have not already taken oath; a man of honor will stand by the truth as it appears to him, even though that will incur the anger of a powerful neighbor. After the verdict has been pronounced the suitors are morally bound to enforce it. Nowadays that is much easier than it used to be; if there is danger of serious fighting the sheriff will come to their help with his Norman followers. This new king keeps the peace with a heavy hand. It is the best thing about him.

All the same, a suitor in any court is taking sides all the time, and that may sometimes mean taking sides against the bulk of his neighbors. It is unpleasant, though of course it is also honorable. A free man should always be ready to bear arms against evildoers, whether domestic criminals or foreign invaders. Freedom and fighting are intertwined; you cannot have one without the other.

After this last piece of advice Godric mounts his cheap and comfortable hackney, and Edward sets off half a length behind him on a pony. (No Norman would make room in his stable for any of Godric's horses, if he were to find it straying ownerless on the road.) For this dull meeting of the unimportant hundred court Godric rides unarmed; though for an annual meeting of the shire court he is warned to bring all his equipment, so that the fyrd of Berkshire can be numbered and valued.

Though Godric talks a good deal about his honor as a free socman and his willingness to fight for it, he has been lucky in avoiding the battlefields. When the Norman Earls of Hereford and Norfolk revolted against King William in 1075, the fyrd of Berkshire was ordered to muster in arms, though later it was dismissed without fighting. Godric has never used his arms, though he has been trained to use them.

He has been trained to fight on foot, with a long two-handed ax. There is not much skill in that, except for the elementary trick of feinting at the head and then striking sideways at the feet; the elementary defense against this is to jump high over the sweeping blade, and counter at your enemy's bent back before he can recover. But Godric can handle his great five-foot ax with ease and familiarity; he is never pulled off balance by the impetus of his own stroke.

His ax has been in the family for generations, probably since an ancestor took it from a dead Viking during the wars of King Alfred. His steel helmet is also an heirloom. But his excellent mail shirt, of supple links of steel, was made for him quite recently, chiefly at the expense of his neighbors. In Berkshire at least, though we cannot speak so certainly of other shires, every five hides of arable land is supposed to send one man to the fyrd. Godric enjoys fyrd service, and he has inherited some sound arms. Normally he serves for his own three hides and those of two neighbors, who supply his mail and his rations. This was one of the many regulations, devised by some long-dead king, which took it for granted that English landholders would co-operate reasonably, without quarreling or standing on the letter of their rights; the duties of Norman knights had to be laid down in greater detail.

Godric can ride quite adequately along a road; no horse would put him down on the flat. But he has been taught to consider it un-English, perhaps flighty and undignified, to fight on horseback. If he were to meet a foe unexpectedly round a corner of the road, he would at once dismount. He rides only when traveling. Therefore, he has never tried to master the Norman skill of taking a horse wherever a man can go, across mountains and through bogs and deep rivers, and he does not fuss very much over the condition of his horse's back or legs.

Edward also can ride adequately on the flat. He wishes he could ride like a Norman, but at home there is no one to teach him. One day, when he is grown up, he will owe military service to the King or to some other lord. Military service is the mark of a free man, and if he always puts up money to hire someone else to do it for him his ancient and distinguished family will lose status. But at the present day no one wants a mailed axman. On a horse he cannot keep up with those fantastic Norman riders, and on foot he cannot march ten miles in his heavy mail. Edward will have to practice the bow, or learn to throw javelins; then he will be of some military value as a light-armed scout.

Meanwhile they have before them this meeting of the hundred court. Probably there will be very little business, but certainly there will be endless formalities. The sheriff's deputy is a decent Englishman, who sees to it that every plea is repeated exactly as it should be. The defendant must answer the charge in full, contradicting in exactly the same form all that has been alleged against him. At the end A, the accuser, will have sworn that on a certain day at a certain place B, the accused, did X. B will have sworn that he never did X, either on that day at that place or at any other time or place. If either of them should get one part of the formula wrong, then the suit is ended. But if they have recited their lessons correctly the suitors will be faced with a complete contradiction.

There are several ways in which the suitors may arrive at a verdict. One method they would never dream of trying: they will not hear evidence from third parties to find out what actually happened. The third parties would resent being put on oath against their will; only the King, or his own immediate lord, may compel a free man to take oath, and even he had better not do it too often. Besides, if the witnesses should consent to be sworn, everyone would assume that they would swear anything to help their kindred or friends.

But it is also assumed that a man with reputable friends is more likely to be in the right than a nobody. One way of settling a matter in dispute is for each party to muster his oath helpers. These do not swear that they know, of their own knowledge, that their man is in the right; they swear that he is the sort of man whose assertion ought to be believed. Then the other party musters his oath helpers, and after all the oaths have been sworn they are weighed. The oath of a nobleman is much heavier than that of a peasant; a free socman of good family comes somewhere in between.

Yet this excellent method of settling disputes is falling into disuse now that so many eminent men are Normans, who don't hold with it. If two Normans disagree on a point of fact, they decide it by fighting; either with blunt weapons under strict rules if it is not very important, or by mortal combat, mounted, with lance and sword if they are really in earnest. Thus a respectable Englishman may ask his lord to take oath, and get the answer that he ought to be fighting a duel instead of swearing.

There is one other method of deciding criminal cases: by ordeal. The usual ordeal was to grasp a piece of hot iron and afterwards show your hand unmarked; or perhaps to be thrown, bound, into a pond and not be drowned. In other words, a miracle was always necessary to prove the innocence of the accused. It seems unfair that no one ever called on God to demonstrate by a miracle that the accused was guilty.

Why did people go on believing in the fairness of the ordeal when the accused always failed the test? There is a simple answer. First, the accused was acquitted or found guilty by the common opinion of the suitors, who decided the case, without hearing evidence, by what they knew of the man personally. If, after he had been found guilty, he still refused to admit his guilt, he might be allowed a last chance at the ordeal. Of course he failed, and nobody was surprised, for they had all thought him to be guilty before the ordeal began. It is possible that the suitors had been mistaken, but that can happen to a jury at the present day.

On this occasion we need not inquire into what happened at the hundred court, which in any case had very limited powers of punishment. If anyone has done wrong he will be remanded to the shire court; after each civil suit has been decided the defeated party will lodge an appeal. One might say that the whole day had been a waste of time, except that it kept the local landholders up to the mark and reminded them that the King held them responsible for law and order in the hundred.

Godric and Edward have not entirely wasted their day. They have met their neighbors and got to know the local deputy for the sheriff. Godric gave him, discreetly, a few silver pennies, and in future will not be asked to provide, at an inconvenient time, the dozen hens and six dozen eggs that his land ought to send annually to help feed the King. Many English estates were burdened with these small foodrents, which were as much of a nuisance to collect as to provide. By the eleventh century they went no farther than the sheriff, who paid annually a lump sum, called his "farm," to the King. Most landholders found it prudent to give the sheriff a little more than his bare due. The sheriff, who represents the King in every branch of local administration, can make himself a great nuisance if he takes a dislike to you. Eighty years later, during the reign of King Henry II, "the sheriff's aid" will have become so like a regular tax that the King will try, unsuccessfully, to take it for himself.

The court remains in session until after midday, far too late for the suitors to get home for dinner. Godric and Edward brought bread and cold beef on their saddles, and a leather bottle of ale. All the suitors picnic together in the open air, which gives a last occasion for gossip until they meet again at the next hundred court. As they sit on the ground a shower of rain falls, but they do not move to shelter. They hardly notice rain, because they all habitually wear a great many thick clothes, indoors and out. Then they ride slowly in the direction of their homes, to get in before supper but not too long before.

On their way Godric and Edward watch to see that their peasants are doing their work properly; though at this season, just before harvest, not much needs attention. With stonebows and slings the children are scaring birds off the ripe grain; the men are looking over their sickles and other tools before the reaping. The crops stand high, and all the men contrive to look busy. Godric is not interested in new and progressive agriculture; his land has been in the family for more than three hundred years, and he does not wish to alter anything he saw done when he was a boy. Everyone knows that you ought to sow seed brought from a distance, and that the plowing must be deep and thorough. That is enough. This new-fangled business of laying drains and spreading lime he leaves to newfangled Norman lords.

While the men are out of the way at the hundred court, the women of the household have been busy in the hall. The harvest will begin very soon, and after that will come the slaughter and salting of the winter meat. By Michaelmas, in September, all the produce of the year, animal and vegetable, should be gathered in. But reaping, binding, and gleaning take all the available hands on the place, even the women and children, and the harvesters must be fed. All this morning Godgifu and Edith have supervised the turning out of the kitchen in preparation for the hard work ahead. The kitchen, a little shed standing by itself to lessen danger from fire, is sooty and smelly. Godgifu nearly arranged to have it burned down and build a new one, but on second thought she decided that the present cabin might last another year. Nevertheless, tables must be scrubbed, cooking pots scoured, and hearths cleaned. Soon they will be turning out vast quantities of beans and bacon for men sweating in the fields.

Most of the arable land in the village is held by individual peasants, but about a third of it is Godric's own demesne. That is worked for him by the villagers, in payment for their holdings. As a rule they work at their own expense, bringing their own food; but at harvest time their wives will be working beside them, and all must be fed from the hall kitchen.

The butchering and salting of the winter's beef and pork will also need clean and unencumbered tables. In the autumn, when the grass has ceased to grow, the horses and the breeding stock of other animals will have to be fed on costly hay or on husks saved from the last threshing. Most of the young stock will be slaughtered; every beast must then be slit down the middle and the two halves salted. Salt beef and salt pork can keep sweet for several months, though by the spring they will not be very appetizing. During the whole winter no one will eat fresh meat, except for birds and small animals caught in the woods. Of course, they would all like very much to eat fresh venison, but the deer which browse on their young crops belong to the King, and the penalty for poaching is so savage that it is not considered worth risking.

In theory the punishment includes frightful mutilations, which cannot fail to end in death since there is no skilled medical care. In practice the King wants money rather than blood, and would rather take Godric's land than harm him physically. But if Godric were to be caught killing deer, or encouraging his men to kill them, he would at the least be reduced to beggary. Nobody makes a habit of poaching except a few desperate men, already outlawed, who lurk in the greenwood.

This is not exactly a new law; from time immemorial all deer have belonged to the King. But the Normans enforce this law more efficiently than was ever done in the past, as they do everything more efficiently. The peasants complain of it as a novel tyranny.

On the other hand, Normans never hang anybody. In England capital punishment has been abolished. Some

69

complain that this is a change in the old English law of King Edward, which at his coronation King William swore to uphold. But Godric, who prides himself on his skill in the law, holds that this is a vulgar error. By the ancient custom of the English, every man was lawful or not, and any man who had put himself outside the law was at the King's mercy. The holy King Edward was accustomed to hang every outlaw he could catch, and especially poachers, unless indeed he forgave them altogether, to the annoyance of his honest subjects. King William ordains that their eyes be put out, which gives them time to repent and be absolved by a priest before they die of the ensuing blood poisoning. In either case these men have been punished by royal justice; the gravity of the punishment has always been at the discretion of the King.

By dinnertime the kitchen is getting into shape, and the ladies may leave the servants to finish the work. As a rule dinner is the chief event of the day, but since Godric is absent they will reserve their main energies for supper. Of course, at dinner there must be plenty to eat for all comers. That is necessary for Godric to maintain his station in life. It is a religious obligation that every husband must provide resources to keep up his station in life, and that a wife must see it kept up. The alternative is to abandon everything and go to live as a hermit, leaving your family to fend for themselves. But to scrape and live thriftily is unthinkable and disgraceful.

When Godgifu gets back to the hall she finds a peddler, and two respectable peasants who are on their way from the west to visit their Norman lord in Sussex. The peddler is a foreigner, which makes him interesting. His pack contains silken thread from far away in Greece, which he will sell to convents for their embroidery; he bought it at one of the great fairs in the Rhineland. His brand of German can be understood by Englishmen who listen carefully. His tales of the wars of northern France would be more interesting to a Norman, but he can also describe the great churches they are building beside the Rhine. He is on his way from Southampton to the Midlands, and will not stay the night. A pity; his stories might have amused Godric.

At dinnertime a good many peasants come in, men who have been working near by. Some are serfs who have been putting in an extra day on the demesne, getting gear ready for harvest. If Godric were to consult a lawyer, he would be told there is no limit to the work he may demand from a serf; a serf is only a slave by another name, and all his time belongs to his owner. Of course, Godric himself knows better. The custom of the manor governs what his serfs must do for him; if he were to demand more he would meet passive resistance, and there are no police. But before harvest all serfs expect to put in a few extra days, just as they expect to be given a good dinner in compensation. They will eat beef, which they would not get at home, and the ale will be stronger and more plentiful. The other peasants are men who work permanently about the house, without cultivating any land of their own. They are better fed than any villager, and in winter they keep warmer; but all their lives they must do what they are told and they rarely have an opportunity to marry. Ordinary peasants envy their comfort and despise their lack of self-respect.

Young Wulf has again forgotten to come home to dinner. He went out on foot in the morning "to see how the sheep are doing," and probably wandered off into the woods. Usually he remembers to carry bread and cheese in his wallet, and any peasant for miles round would be proud to offer hot porridge to a Godricson; so Godgifu is not at all worried at his absence. He is a bit of an absent-minded poet, but then, so are a great many other wellborn Englishmen.

Godgifu and Edith sit alone at the head of the table, shut off from their companions by the empty places belonging to the missing members of the family. Dinner in this depleted household is cold meat and cheese, with a great deal of bread. But even barley bread and oatcake are the food of the well-to-do—much more pleasant than the cold greenstuff the really poor eat when their supplies are running short before harvest. No one complains.

Of course, there is plenty of ale. The peddler puts away an astonishing quantity, considering that he intends to walk another ten miles before sunset. But it does not make him drunk; it only makes his tales of foreign parts more vivid and amusing. When the meal is over Godgifu is sorry to see the last of him.

After Godgifu has given the signal to rise, the men go back to their work and the travelers take up their journey. All have eaten enough bread and cheese and beef to last them until dinner tomorrow, enough to send any modern

man to sleep for a few hours. But their stomachs are accustomed to plenty of food in the middle of the day, and it does not hinder them from working.

While the maids are clearing the table and scouring the beechwood platters, Godgifu goes off to her bower to continue her needlework. She would like to make fine embroidery, a craft she learned from the nuns when she was a little girl, but there is so much household linen to be mended and set in order that she never has time for anything else. Besides, her eyes are not as keen as they were twenty years ago, and there are no spectacles, no oculists.

The truth is that Godric cannot really afford to live in the fashion he does—feeding all comers and turning so much of his grain into ale. Godgifu has to pinch and mend to keep things going. In the old days silver did not go off the place every year, in payment of dues to the lord and of *geld* to the King. It may have been owed, but no one insisted on payment. This new king cannot be put off with promises, and his subordinates never let things slide. Yet Godric cannot alter the manner of his life. He is a free Englishman of noble birth, and if he began to live like a poor man he would be shamed. He cannot sink into the middle class, for there is no middle class; in Berkshire everyone is either a nobleman or a peasant. Godgifu hopes that she will be able to keep the estate going during her husband's lifetime. One day Edward will have to serve a lord for wages; Edith will probably make a good marriage, because of her noble descent;

Wulf will have to look after himself, and he is already laying plans for the future.

This afternoon Edith need not help her mother in the bower, a detached timber building where ladies may take refuge from the noise and occasional drunkenness of the hall. It is a room reserved for ladies only, and if a strange man should blunder into it Godric would be justified in chasing him out with the great ax. But Edith must still make herself useful. She must see that the maids leave everything sweet and clean; for cleanliness in the hall, as well as in personal clothing, is an essential badge of gentility. For one thing, since cleanliness is so hard to achieve, it proves you have plenty of servants.

After Edith has done her duty she may walk in the meadows and admire the sunset until it is time for supper. She seldom goes riding; in fact, she can hardly sit a horse. But she is permitted occasional solitude that a more important lady could never enjoy.

She knows that by next summer she will be married, though her parents have not yet chosen her husband. Within riding distance there are half-a-dozen English socmen of adequate estate, and it is sure to be one of them. Men ride about a good deal, and she has seen them all at dinner in her father's hall. Unfortunately, men usually leave their women at home, so she still does not know which of these socmen are bachelors. She has very little idea of what she will do with herself after she is married. She has never learned how to read, and she does not care for embroidery. Managing a crowded hall, and presently a crowded nursery, will fill most of her time. She gets on well with cows; she hopes her future husband will keep a good dairy herd.

Hers will be a dull life, with a fair amount of worry in it. Women worry over money, while their husbands are striking noble attitudes or spending too much on their personal pleasures. But if she can keep her family solvent she will occupy a responsible and respected position; and there must be some pleasure in marriage or so many people would not undertake it. She expects to outlive her husband, because that is what usually happens. She has already made up her mind about how she will live as a widow. She will lodge in some prosperous religious community, not as a nun but as a lay boarder. In the chapel she will hear as much good music as anyone could want, and she will pass the rest of her time chatting by the fire with wellborn nuns or fellow boarders. She does not care for the society of men. What she really likes about marriage is that it will probably lead to widowhood.

Wulf has been sitting very still in the shade of an oak, watching young rabbits at play in an open glade, when suddenly he becomes aware that he is very hungry. As soon as his hand moves to his wallet the rabbits naturally run into their burrows, but there are still the bracken and the sky to gaze at. White clouds moving across the blue sky give it a look of the open sea; the bracken, seen from ground level, suggests an impenetrable forest. So, as Wulf munches his bread and cheese, he begins to think about the ends of the earth. As soon as he is grown up he will go off to the ends of the earth to earn his living. He has it all planned out.

He is the only member of the family who dislikes Normans. They have never done him any harm, but he resents their swaggering horsemanship and the contempt with which they regard all Englishmen. He would very much like to hit a Norman with a two-handed battle-ax. What a pity that splendid battle at Hastings was fought and lost some years before he was born. If only he, Wulf, had been there it might have gone the other way, and then everything would be different and better. Harold Godwinson was a baseborn usurper, a rebel against the saintly King Edward; he must have been a wicked man because Father, who can remember him, says so. Perhaps the English might have chosen a more honest leader, and then they would still be as proud and independent as in the days of King Alfred, when his own ancestors were important thanes and not mere socmen. But there is still a land where English axmen frequently wage war on Norman knights—a land very far off, but he has been told how to get there.

The quickest way to get there is to ride right through France and Italy; but both these countries swarm with Normans, and to travel overland always costs money. There is another way, slower and longer, but on it any able-bodied warrior may work his passage without fee.

When Wulf is fully grown he will demand arms from his father, who will surely give what he asks to a younger son leaving home to seek his fortune. Then he has only to sail to Flanders, a cheap and easy voyage. In Bruges he will find a Swedish ship, for Bruges is one of the favorite harbors of the Northmen. He will work his passage to Sweden, and then start the great journey "south-overland." On that year-long journey he will find no innkeepers asking payment for board and lodging; supplies are taken by force from wandering savages. Up one Russian river he will travel by boat, and after a short portage, row down another to its mouth. Then he will coast along a warm southern sea until he reaches the great imperial city of Constantinople, where the Emperor maintains a bodyguard of noble ax-bearing Northmen. It is common knowledge that many defeated survivors of Hastings ended their days there.

Constantinople has captured his imagination. He has never met anyone who has seen it, but he has heard plenty of accounts at third hand. Every year merchants from Germany visit the great city to buy its silks and carved ivories. They have spread the story all over the West. The mighty Emperor sits on a throne of pure gold in the shade of an artificial golden tree. By machinery, or perhaps by magic, golden birds flutter and sing in the branches of this tree. By the same mysterious influence, golden lions lift their heads and roar as they watch the base of the throne. The Emperor sits at his ease, because all this wealth is protected by honest Northern heroes, the famous Varangian Guard. The Varangians will be glad to recruit Wulf, an English poet and a nobleman who can trace his descent from Woden. In Constantinople, he will wear gilded armor and carry a jeweled ax as he patrols the Emperor's palace on foot. But sometimes the Emperor leads out his men against the invading Normans from Italy, and then Wulf will have a chance to fight against the foe who conquered the English at Hastings; he will fight on foot, with his ax, in the old English fashion. His silly old parents suggest that he should learn how to ride like a Norman, and then seek wages as a knight. How much grander to walk the streets of the greatest city in the world, dressed in splendid robes and bearing gilded arms, respected as the oath-bound companion of the mighty Emperor! When he is too old for campaigning he will come home rich and astonish the neighbors. The Emperor is famous for the costly presents he gives to his companions. Of course, he chooses Englishmen and other Northerners for his bodyguard, for with all the world to recruit from he knows that they are the most faithful battle companions to be found.

Or perhaps Wulf will be killed, in some hopeless last stand under the imperial standard. In some ways that would be even more satisfactory. Every man is going to die some day, and English poets respect the man who fought on when he might have fled even more than they do the victorious hero. Normans, on the other hand, never suppose that anyone can beat them, and go into every battle expecting victory. Perhaps that is one reason why Normans now rule England.

Wulf murmurs to himself some lines from *The Battle of Maldon*. There are many stirring old English poems about battles, and many of them deal with honorable defeats. Most of the Englishmen who composed good poetry took a gloomy view of life.

It is a pity that Wulf, with his intelligence and his alert imagination, never learned how to read and write. He is rather sorry about it now, though no one would undertake to teach a boy as old as ten. When he was smaller, odd jobs about the farm kept him busy. Besides, their local parish priest does not teaching promising boys, though that is the custom in many parishes.

Wulf has learned by heart a number of English poems, and he delights in declaiming them as he marks the beat of the verse on a harp. But the number of those who enjoy his recitals grows less every year. Old English poetry was composed in a complicated, artificial language, in which nearly every common object was described under another name: "warhorses of the waves" for ships, and so on. Under the Normans everyone who writes for posterity writes in Latin or French, and the only English in common use is the bare colloquial speech of the peasants. If Wulf lives to old age no one will be able to follow him when he sings of Brunanburh or Maldon. But he refuses to recognize the fact. There may yet be an English revival.

This attitude seems so natural to us, by analogy with modern Poles and Irishmen, that we suppose it must have been almost universal. In fact, it was rare. After Wulf has grown up and gone oversea there will be little discontent in Berkshire. One reason is that Normans are not exclusive. Any free man who will learn to ride and to speak French is welcome to become a knight, so that young Englishmen have an outlet for their ambition. But there is a certain amount of discontent, and some Normans are aware of it; as late as the reign of King Henry II, the Norman Abbot of Battle will warn all Normans to close their ranks against the threat of English rebellion.

Wulf does not plan, when he is older, to free England from the Norman yoke. He would like to free Berkshire, but he does not see how it could be done. For other Englishmen, outlanders from strange shires, he feels no sympathy. He would like to fight Normans, but that can be done in Greece as well as anywhere else. He is not so eccentric as to be a patriot; his own self-esteem is what matters to him.

But he has been dreaming for a long time, and he must get home before supper. So that the day shall not be completely wasted he walks through the arable fields on his way home. He will be able to report that the harvest is nearly ready, and that the crops have been properly tended.

Meanwhile, Godric and Edward, riding home from the hundred court with two neighbors, are perfectly content with the political situation. They remember that they can trace descent from a king's thane who won fame in the wars of King Alfred. He held a great deal more than three hides of land, but no enemy has defrauded Godric of his rightful inheritance. It has been divided and subdivided among the kindred, until three hides was all that came to Godric. But three hides is about the minimum that anyone can live on unless he works with his own hands, which would be a disgrace in such a noble family. So it must all go to Edward when Godric dies. Luckily primogeniture and entail are all the fashion among their Norman neighbors. It may be hard on Wulf, but a line must be drawn somewhere.

No Norman has taken anything from Godric. He pays more in tax, not because the assessment is higher but because the taxes are collected more rigorously. But in return, King William enforces firm peace; Godric has never been compelled to defend his land in arms, either against invaders or against casual brigands. He is still a free man, with exactly the rights and duties his father enjoyed. He is entitled, and indeed compelled, to carry the ancestral battle-ax when the King summons the warriors of Berkshire. He keeps his rightful place as a free suitor in the law courts.

He has not yet noticed that his social position is declining. His alleged descent from Woden, his certain descent from a royal house of the old Heptarchy, mean nothing to the new ruling class. In the eyes of the Norman barons no one may rank as a gentleman unless he can speak French. Edward, or perhaps his son, may learn a foreign language and adopt foreign ways; otherwise the Godricsons will soon be regarded as no more than prosperous free peasants. When they visit a Norman castle they will be seated with the lower orders.

But so far nothing has been decided. Norman noblemen did not inquire closely into pedigrees; few of their own pedigrees would bear examination. If Edward chooses to conform to the new state of affairs he will be accepted everywhere, provided he keeps hold of enough land to live without working. Many of the respected baronial families of the later Middle Ages were of English descent, and in time they came to be proud of it. The social barrier exists only in Wulf's imagination.

Meanwhile the family is gathering for supper; and since dinner was a scratch meal in the absence of the head of the house, supper will be the chief event of the day. Like most other English socmen, Godric takes his food seriously.

He has brought home two guests, fellow suitors from the hundred court who will stop a night in his hall on their way to talk business with the sheriff at Reading. They also ate a cold dinner from their wallets after the hundred court had adjourned, and they must be properly impressed by Godric's lavish table. There are also a couple of peddlers, who eat with the farm workers, and a respectable merchant of York, on his way to Southampton with a pack train, who will sit with the family.

Before supper Godric and his family put on better clothes, since this will be a formal occasion. They also wash their faces and hands. But all the same they are not very much cleaner, for under their fine clothes they still keep on their workaday garments. Godric and the boys wear fine supertunics, Godgifu and Edith mantles over their gowns. There can be no question of heating a bath, for all the servants are busy in the kitchen.

Supper, when it comes, is almost another dinner: roast pork, roast beef, and fine wheaten bread. Everyone fills up with meat and grain, for there are no vegetables. Greenstuff is the food of paupers, and roots are fit only to feed cattle. The drinking horns are kept constantly filled with ale, but no wine is served. Wine is un-English.

When they have eaten enough the ladies retire to their bower, but the men sit on over their ale. To begin with, a harp is passed from hand to hand and everyone is supposed to sing at least one song. Wulf contributes a long poem, a traditional battle-piece with embellishments of his own composition. The merchant recites a Flemish lay which is new to the rest of the company. The others show willingness by singing something short and familiar. Nobody is very interested, except when it is his own turn to perform; but it is the right thing to do at that time of the day, and they feel that they are carrying on an ancient ritual.

The servants and peasants are too shy to perform, though the harp is scrupulously handed down to the bottom table. It is still too early for bed, and everyone would like more ale. This is traditionally the time to discuss politics.

Godric makes heavy conversation, chiefly for the edification of his sons. The merchant, who knows the news of the Midlands, plays up as well as he can. But it is all a little unreal. There was a time when kings reigned because men like Godric supported them, and made way for some rival when they lost that support. But not since Hastings. King William reigns because he claims the three indispensable qualifications: he was the appointed heir of his predecessor, he has been crowned by the

Church with the assent of his subjects, and he has the military force to defend his inheritance. Anyone who possesses this third qualification finds the first two added to him.

But the King depends on the loyalty of Norman horsemen, and cares nothing for the sentiments of English ax-bearers. Even if Godric were expert with his great ax, and now he is a little past warfare, he would still have no political importance. The sheriff finds him useful as a suitor in the shire and hundred courts, his lord would be poorer without the dues he pays punctually; but so long as knights dominate the battlefields he will remain a subject, of no military value.

The ladies retired, as they should, before the men began to get drunk. The men, as they should, drink rather more ale than they can carry. But the glory is departed.

III · THE LONDONERS

Olaf Haconson lives with his wife and three children in London, down by the river. When anyone asks him his occupation (and Norman officials are great ones for making lists and finding out how everyone earns a living), he describes himself as a ropemaker and ship's fitter. That is what he does nowadays more often than he does anything else, so the answer is broadly true. But all his neighbors know that he has retired from the navy. In 1065 he was a young *butsecarle*, a professional sea fighter, on one of the ships King Edward maintained in London River.

In the spring of 1066 he sailed with the fleet to defend England from Norman invasion. With his shipmates he had taken oath to serve Harold Godwinson, the new half-Danish king whom all London followed. But before the Normans put to sea in the autumn, the English ships had run short of provisions and returned to their London base; so there was no fighting in the Channel. Then it became known that King Harold had been killed at Hastings, and according to English ideas an oath of fidelity was binding only while both parties were alive. Back on shore, Olaf took his two-handed Danish ax and helped to swell the militia of London. At first the Londoners planned to set up the infant Edgar Atheling as king, but they could not agree on who should rule as regent in his name. In the late autumn they made terms with Duke William, who has been recognized as King of England since the Londoners crowned him on Christmas Day, 1066. But London made terms; it did not surrender at discretion. Ever since, the King has handled it carefully and left it in enjoyment of wide liberties. London is no mean city, and Olaf is proud of his burgess-right.

Olaf's wife is named Emma, and their three children are Harold, aged fourteen, Matilda, aged twelve, and Robert, aged ten. Their names show that they come of mixed race, though the system of using ancestral names is breaking down and names do not always show the whole truth.

Olaf's father and mother both called themselves Danes. His mother believed that her family had come over from Denmark with King Sweyn, father of the mighty Canute; Hacon claimed that his ancestors had been Vikings who accepted Christianity and settled down in London in the days of King Alfred. By this time they took no interest in what was happening in Denmark across the sea, but they felt some kinship with the Danes of East Anglia.

Emma believes she is of Mercian descent, or perhaps West Saxon; certainly English of some kind, long settled in London. Olaf insisted that their eldest son should be christened Harold after his own dead lord. It is a noncommittal name, which might be either English or Danish. "Matilda" is by origin Flemish, just as "Emma" is Norman. But the London-born Emma was named after the queen who had been the mother of King Edward the Confessor, at a time when the name was fashionable in England as being at the same time foreign and vaguely romantic. The name "Robert" is also foreign and romantic, and in cosmopolitan London conveys no claim to Norman blood. When the child is grown up he will be known as Robert Olafson, or Robert fitzOlaf, a mingling of languages typical of London.

At home by the fireside the family speak the Mercian dialect of English, which is the common speech of London. They can understand Danish and Flemish, and any other Germanic tongue. Olaf claims in addition that he can understand French, though Frenchmen do not often understand what he says in reply. They know the meaning of some of the Latin prayers they hear often in church, though they cannot say anything new in Latin. None of them can read or write.

Their social position is difficult to define. In strict legal theory every Londoner has a *were* (the money value set on his life) of one hundred shillings, which is the same as that of a churl, a free peasant. But that does not mean that most burgesses are poor; it is a concession granted by the King, or perhaps by some ancient king. In the same way no Londoner can be compelled to stand trial by the newfangled method of battle, or to plead in any court outside London. This was all part of the treaty made with King William. London is an important place.

What makes London important is that it is still surrounded by its strong Roman wall, which is defended, if necessary, by a warlike militia. When this militia is summoned by the great bell of St. Paul's, Olaf is there in his mail shirt and helmet, with his great ax balanced on his shoulder. He cannot be called a knight, for he is not especially good on a horse; but he is one of the men whom the King has in mind when he addresses a writ to the "barons" of London, using the word baron in its ancient sense to mean any free warrior.

Olaf is now in his middle forties, and when the warriors of London march out on campaign he will be left behind to guard the famous wall. His eldest son, Harold, is still a bit too young for military service; though in a crisis he also would be on the wall, dropping stones or pouring boiling water.

Yet Olaf has not always dodged active service, as he did by good luck in 1066. During the early reign of King William he slipped away oversea, to Bruges, according to his own story—perhaps to Dublin as many of his neighbors say. He was away for three years, and he came home with a wallet full of silver. It is likely, though no one can prove it, that he sailed on Viking cruise.

Olaf never talks of what he did on his travels. No one has the bad manners to inquire into the subject. Nowadays he pays his taxes promptly, and earns his living openly and honestly. Every day he goes down to the wharfs with a coil of rope over his shoulder. The rope he makes is not especially strong, not nearly so good as the cordage imported from the Baltic; but he is expert at repairing damaged rigging, and even damaged steering oars, which are very tricky to mend. If a ship from oversea has been in a little trouble from a storm, or from a brush with another, more heavily armed ship, her master will be glad of Olaf's help. Of course, if the ship had been gravely damaged it would not be in London River at all; it would be at the bottom of the shallow North Sea. So Olaf never finds a task that would be too much for his self-taught skill.

He keeps away from the shipbuilders, a clannish lot who seldom accept any new worker who is not himself the son of a shipbuilder. But not many new ships are built in the port of London, not nearly so many as come from oversea to trade. There is not much big timber suitable for shipbuilding within reach of the city; during every past disturbance the neighboring forests were heavily cut for firewood, and now they are reserved for the burgesses' hunting. Most English ships are built in the Kent or Sussex ports, or on Southampton Water.

But foreigners nearly always need running repairs before they can set out for home; and the more important communities of foreign merchants have their own wharfs on the river, where they may always be found. There is a busy quay where the ships of Rouen are tied up. It has nothing to do with the Norman Conquest; merchants from the Seine were using it before the time of King Edward. They bring freestone for building, wine, and luxuries from Paris, besides a special fat fish for the pleasure of the King or the Queen. This fish may have been a porpoise or a dolphin or even a whale; its Latin name is ambiguous and we do not know what it was called in French. It was so rare in English waters that it was reserved for the royal table; but the King's household paid an honest price for it.

There is an even more important wharf, used only by "the men of the Emperor." The Holy Roman Empire is a very wide realm, extending throughout Germany and Lotharingia from the shores of the Baltic perhaps as far south as Rome. But in this connection "the men of the Emperor" are goldsmiths and jewelers of the lower Rhine. Wonderful things reach them from Constantinople at the end of the long river route; they embellish them until they are even more beautiful and then bring them to London by sea. London is the terminus of that incredibly long trade route, the only market in England where you can buy precious and beautiful things. We know of eight goldsmiths in London who worked for King William, and there may have been others. At that time there is no record of a goldsmith in any other English town. King William's silver pennies are struck in a great many places, but all the dies for them are made in London, where the King's officials can enforce the correct standard of value.

"The men of the Emperor" who trade in London come

from only a few German towns; merchants from other imperial towns might not get justice when they arrived here. These traders are protected by the treaties their home cities have concluded with the City of London. Londoners may go the other way and sell their goods safely when they reach the Rhine, though few of them do; for the only produce of England valued in Germany is fine needlework. All this has been arranged between the merchants of London and the merchants of the Rhine, without help from any emperor or king. London is strong enough to conduct her own foreign policy.

Of course, this can be done only because London governs herself and can act as a unit. Unfortunately, the new king has impaired the freedom of the Londoners, though even in these degenerate days they still enjoy a measure of liberty. The basis of their power was their mighty wall, which they might, if they wished, hold even against the King. Now these castle-building Normans have impaired its integrity. Towards the east, where the wall comes down to the Thames, the King has built a fortress, the famous Tower of London. The *motte* is steep and moated by an inlet from the Thames, the eastern part of the bailey is an angle of the wall itself, and the fortress has gates to the east and to the west. So long as the *motte* is held by a faithful Norman garrison, the King's knights may ride in from the open country, and through the west gate penetrate the streets of the city. Out to the west there is another smaller fort, known as Baynard's Castle from the name of the Norman lord who holds it. That also sits astride the wall.

Yet both these castles are held for King William. So long as the Londoners remain loyal to the King, they may defy any other lord, Norman or English. In fact, these castles actually strengthen the wall against outside attack. But the militia of London must hold the greater length of it.

They can do that quite well. Every able-bodied burgess has an ax or at least a spear; the more prosperous own swords. Olaf is better equipped than most, with the big two-handed ax and the fine byrnie, or mail shirt, that were given to him long ago by good King Edward. His mail is very old-fashioned, reaching down only to his hips so that his legs may move nimbly on the deck of a ship. Modern mail, intended to be worn by horsemen, comes down to the calves and is cumbrous for fighting on foot. Olaf keeps his old byrnie greased and free from rust; his helmet is obviously proof against sword strokes. At the muster he swings his ax with an air. He is a veteran warrior and everyone can see it. When military affairs are under discussion the others keep silent while Olaf gives his opinion.

In time of peace the folkmoot of all the Londoners meets only three times a year, chiefly to hear the commands of the Norman portreeve, or sheriff. But the sheriff cannot tax them. How much they shall pay to the King has been settled in advance, and they may collect it among themselves by any method they please. So long as the total is correct the sheriff may not inquire into who paid how much. That makes for unfairness, naturally; rich merchants get together, and those least able to pay bear the heaviest burden. A Norman with no family ties among the burgesses probably would divide the amount more fairly. But that the Londoners have the right to tender their own "farm," is a cherished symbol of freedom. They would all rather put up with a little unfairness than have a stranger prying into their affairs, either a Norman or an outlander from some other part of England.

When all the Londoners have assembled in arms before St. Paul's they feel very proud of their mighty city, even though the muster normally ends with their hearing the King's commands transmitted through the sheriff. But this folkmoot, meeting only three times in the year, cannot manage all the business of a thriving city. Once a week, every Monday, the aldermen of the twenty-four wards assemble under the portreeve, in the hustings court.

Olaf still experiences a mild thrill whenever he hears that name. All Londoners recognize it as something typical of their city, but only the Danes among them know that it is in origin Danish. There may have been something like the hustings court before the first Vikings sailed to Britain, for Londoners like to suppose that their city has existed without a break since the Romans lived in it; but real self-government must have come in with the Danish settlement. On those Monday mornings the important business of the city is transacted.

The aldermen from each ward meet in a hall, sitting round the walls on four benches; that proves they are not barbarians, who gather under the open sky to express their opinions by beating their swords against their shields. At this meeting every foreign merchant who comes in peace must produce all his followers and serving-men, so that respectable burgesses may vouch for them. Of course, "foreign" means from outside London; a trader from Bristol or Southampton must comply with the same formalities as a trader from Cologne.

Otherwise there are the same civil and criminal cases as in a shire court. Every important sale must be registered before the hustings, especially sales of land or houses. They take up a lot of time, for Londoners are always buying and selling houses. They may dispose of land without leave from any feudal lord.

London is not yet a commune, a corporate feudal lord. That development will come in the next century. The King appoints the sheriff who commands the militia; the lord of Baynard's Castle leads those burgesses who serve on horseback after the Norman fashion. Even the aldermen who command the contingent from each ward are appointed by the King, though the King cannot have known enough about the burgesses of London to choose out twenty-four as specially worthy of his trust. Once appointed, an alderman usually holds office for life; he is so often succeeded by his son that he may have recommended his successor. Probably the sheriff took soundings among the burgesses of each ward before he put up a list of names to the King. An alderman had to be learned in the law, and rich enough to devote most of his time to public duties. Not many burgesses would be qualified to act as aldermen. Their tenure was often so secure that their wards were named after them: Hacon's ward, Ralph's ward. Other wards were identified by natural features: Aldgate ward, Walbrook ward.

Not every Londoner lived in a ward. Neighboring lords, clerical and lay, employed some man of business to buy and sell for them in the greatest market in England. In accordance with ordinary feudal principles the merchant and his servants would be under the jurisdiction of their employer; for a lord has the duty of maintaining order among his dependents wherever they may dwell. The houses of these servants of outland lords are usually surrounded by a stockade. Other people who may come to live within the stockade will owe suit and service to the lord of the whole enclosure, known as a soc since all within it come under the soc, or jurisdiction, of the same man. Presently London will be riddled with these private socs, ancestors of the Liberties of the later Middle Ages. While they exist they make impossible the policing of the city as a whole, for the sheriff or portreeve of London may not summon the inhabitant of a soc save through his lord. But when the bell of St. Paul's summons the folkmoot, every Londoner must attend, and in commercial affairs the hustings has jurisdiction over all of them. Besides, in strict legal theory a soc ranks only as a private manor court, while the hustings is a shire court, capable of deciding important criminal cases.

But we must not suppose that Olaf passed all his time in the law courts; though since it is the records of these courts that have come down to us, historians sometimes forget that the average man does not often come into conflict with the law. On this particular weekday morning in July 1087, Olaf has his living to earn.

He gets up just before sunrise. Long habit has taught him to wake with the dawn, and one of the advantages of living in a big city is that it is fairly easy to know the time. There are no mechanical clocks; but in monasteries and castles, in any place where someone keeps watch all night, they have hourglasses or waterclocks or colored candles which burn down at a predictable rate. The portreeve of London employs watchmen, who are supposed to patrol the streets all night; it is their duty to arrest anyone found in a public place between curfew and dawn, for every honest man should be at home during the hours of darkness. (Like every other big seaport, London has a few low haunts, but they are open only during daylight.) At certain corners the watch call out the hour, and in such a quiet place as London after dark, a burgess can often tell the time by the sound of the passing watchman's feet.

Olaf has been sleeping, in most of his daytime clothes, on a straw mattress in the loft of his house. His wife, also in most of her clothes, shares the mattress with him. Their children sleep in cozy corners of the main room below.

The loft and the main room make up the whole house, a timber building with its gable facing the street. But Olaf owns a considerable area of ground on both sides and at the far end, for the present inhabitants of London have plenty of room within its Roman walls.

Every ordinary London house has this toft on three

sides, and a burgess would feel himself cheated if he had to manage without it. The bigger and more important houses are set in the middle of their tofts, with a thick hedge all round. They are called burghs, which is the English word for any kind of fortification, from a Roman wall to a thorn fence. Olaf uses most of his toft for growing greenstuff, as a standby in case times should be hard; but in it there are also two flimsy sheds. One contains the hooks to which he fastens strands of flax before twisting them into his rather ill-made ropes. To make a rope, he walks slowly backwards, turning a wooden frame to which three strands are fixed; as they slide through the frame, the finished rope emerges on the side nearest the hooks. It is slow work, but not very difficult; there are people in London who make worse rope than he.

The other shed contains a small brick hearth, intended to burn wood or the more expensive charcoal. There Emma cooks her stew whenever they have meat, which is by no means every day. Their daily bread is bought in small quantities from a professional baker in the next street; Emma can bake quite competently, but she can seldom afford to heat the big brick oven. The cooking-place is well away from the house, because accidental fire is the greatest danger to every householder in London.

Olaf and his sons slept in their shirts and drawers. Emma and Matilda slept in their shifts; they never wear drawers. They all like to be warm at night, though they are resigned to a certain amount of cold during the day; with all the windows shuttered and the doors bolted they have got up a good fug. Emma has one big woolen blanket, which was part of Olaf's kit in the days when he went to sea; otherwise they cover themselves with all their spare clothes, with their broad rain-cloaks on top. They know that the gentry sleep naked, which helps them to keep clean; but it is more important to be warm than to be clean, and at dawn even July can be chilly. Besides, even if they washed thoroughly every day, the gentry would still say they stank; the gentry say that of all burgesses. So why bother to keep clean, in considerable discomfort?

Olaf and his family assemble fully clothed for breakfast—a horn of ale and some crusts of stale bread. Olaf has put on a decent tunic, and over that a seaman's canvas jacket without sleeves. It hangs open in front but it conceals the wallet at his girdle, in which he carries a long and very sharp knife which may be used either for cutting food or for slitting throats. In this jacket, a dirty shirt, and his plain workaday leg bandages, he looks very like a common laborer. His dignity is saved by the fine scarlet cap which covers his shaggy hair. It is clean and new, and it terminates on top in a crest like a cock's. Only a man of some position would wear a cap like that.

After he has drunk his ale, standing, he slings a coil of his own rope over his shoulder and goes out to look for a repair job on a ship newly come to land. He tells Emma that he will be home to dinner, and that if all goes well he will bring home some relish to be eaten with the bread he has already ordered and paid for at the baker's. Matilda can fetch that, and Emma can make the table ready; but his life has been so full of sudden changes that he prefers to do the catering himself. This morning there is no spending money in the house, so Emma cannot waste silver in the market even if she would.

Emma wears a large and floppy kirtle, and a kerchief tied under her chin. Both are woven from wool in its natural color, and made even more dingy by plentiful dirt. Even with a decent linen shift underneath, woven from her husband's flax, Emma looks like a badly filled sack; but she is a respectable married woman, and it would be wrong if she looked attractive.

The two boys wear short tunics and leave their legs bare. Robert is also barefoot and without a girdle, but Harold, halfway to dressing like a man, has clumsy leather shoes and a cheap girdle of rawhide. His wallet is of goat-skin with the hair left on, and his eating knife a blade of soft blunt iron. But strapped to his thigh, hidden by the skirts of his tunic, he carries a sharper little knife. That is very naughty of him. Every free man is entitled to bear arms, but an honest man should never hide his weapon. Yet it gives Harold a strong feeling of self-respect, which is the best reason for going armed. Olaf will deliberately fail to notice it unless he actually scratches himself on the hidden point.

Like her mother, Matilda wears a shapeless kirtle over a smock; but her head is uncovered, with her hair hanging in two plaits as a sign that she is still a child. Her feet are bare, grubby, and calloused. In her young life she has never yet worn shoes.

But after she has eaten her breakfast, she straps under her horny soles little frameworks of wood called pattens;

these will lift her feet a few inches from the filth of the streets. She picks up a rush basket and goes to fetch to-day's bread from the baker.

Shopping must be difficult when the smallest coin minted, the silver penny, is a generous wage for a day's labor. The baker round the corner knows Olaf well, and would willingly give him credit. But Olaf, who has lived through ups and downs, likes to keep his credit in reserve. He prefers to give the baker a few pennies in advance, and settle up when that payment has been exhausted.

Some people make their own small change, cutting the silver penny into four farthings. Such a division is quite legal, and to make it easier one side of the penny bears a large cross. But it is an extravagant way to spend ready money. Four separate farthings received in change seldom weigh as much as one sound penny. Nearly always some wicked man has clipped a broken edge, or "sweated" the farthings by shaking them up in a bag until little slivers of silver rub off. Homemade farthings are not a currency to be given to children for the daily shopping. Matilda carries no money at all.

The baker, who knows her by sight, has her little batch of fresh barley rolls smoking hot and waiting for her. He picks up a notched stick and Matilda lays a similar stick beside it, taking care that the notches correspond. While she watches carefully, he makes another notch in both sticks at once. Matilda may be too much of a child to be trusted in the open street with a whole silver penny, but she knows all about tallies and how to mark them honestly.

Besides, the baker is an honest man. Even if he should not always *feel* honest, the penalties for fraud are too serious to be risked. Any self-governing town will see to that. Inspectors appointed by the portreeve come round at frequent intervals to examine every baker's weights and scales and tallies; if he were caught cheating he would be lucky to escape with a flogging—he might very likely be lynched by an angry mob. Nearly all his customers are burgesses, and within their own city burgesses must deal fairly with one another. The measures of a London weaver, who sells most of his cloth to outlanders, are not often so carefully checked.

When Matilda has her bread, she goes straight home like a dutiful daughter and joins her mother in weeding the lettuces in the toft. She has had her outing for the morning. Woman's place is in the home.

A man's place, on the other hand, is anywhere within his native town. As soon as Harold finished breakfast he went out, soon after his father. He is working for a carpenter, who at the same time teaches him the trade.

We must dismiss from our minds any recollection of the guilds of the later Middle Ages. In 1087 there were guilds, but they had no connection with trade or craftsmanship; they were religious and convivial societies, which paid for Masses for the souls of deceased members and spent any money that remained over on cheery social evenings. Indeed, a Norman of the first generation born in England, explaining the customs of the island to his fellow Frenchmen, translates the English word "guild-house" as "drinking den."

In fact, Harold is serving an apprenticeship. When he has learned the craft of carpentry his master will bring him before the hustings court and vouch for him as a skilled carpenter. But as yet there is no rule that his apprenticeship must continue for seven years, or that at the end of it he will enter a closed fellowship. He will remain a learner until, in his master's opinion, he knows all that can be taught about his craft; and then he will practice it, in competition with his fellows, until he succeeds or fails in a world of free enterprise.

When he is grown up he will rank as a free burgess, unless by great good fortune he becomes one of the twenty-four aldermen. No one except his customers will worry about his status as a carpenter. His voice in folk- and wardmoot will depend on his skill at arms. In the eyes of the law, London, like every other English burgh, is chiefly an assembly of armed men; that it happens also to be the wealthiest market in England is not nearly so important.

One guild was already prominent in the London of 1087: the Knights' Guild, using "knight" in its old English meaning of servingman or mounted messenger. It was said that this guild had been founded in the days of King Edgar; it had certainly received additional privileges from King Edward the Confessor. By Norman times it had become smart and fashionable; among its members were some of the greatest merchants in the city, men who could never be ranked as mounted errand-boys. So perhaps it did not begin as an association of messengers. After all, to be a messenger does not create a great bond with other messengers. A messenger from Devonshire is more likely to join a club of other Devon men in London than a club of outland messengers drawn from every part of England. The guild may have been from the beginning a religious association of laymen, who chose to call themselves the Messengers of God or the Messengers of the Church. By 1087 it had become a social and charitable club, perhaps more or less on the lines of modern Rotary. But though its members were eminent, it was evidently not one of the more important activities in their lives, for within forty years they chose to dissolve it. In 1125 the London guild of knights gave all its lands to the new Priory of the Holy Trinity in Aldgate, in exchange for Masses and other spiritual benefits. As a result of this generous gift Holy Trinity came to own the whole Ward of Portsoken, of which its prior was *ex officio* alderman until the Dissolution of the Monasteries by Henry VIII in 1532.

Thus while Harold is learning to be a carpenter, there are guilds in London (for one of them must have built Guildhall, standing in 1100). But they are either benevolent associations or drinking clubs, and none of them are concerned with the trade of carpentry.

We do not know enough about the economic life of London in 1087 to say whether Harold was paid for making himself useful in his master's shop, or whether he paid his master for teaching him the craft. In later times an apprentice paid a premium, but in return he lived as a member of his master's family. Probably at this early time the two more or less canceled out. Perhaps Harold earns a little pocket money, but Olaf has to maintain him.

All the same, Harold has been settled for life. He will learn how to cleave and to saw and to make firm joints. How much further he will go depends on his own brains.

In the eleventh century most large constructions, except stone castles, would be designed by some carpenter. Bridges were often made entirely of wood; London Bridge, spanning the tidal Thames, must have been a considerable technical achievement. All big halls were roofed with wood, very much in the manner of a ship turned upside down. Only a few very strong castles, such as the famous Tower of London which King William had lately erected, had roofs of vaulted masonry.

The unit of construction must be the height of tall trees growing in the neighborhood. Nobody would move a tree very far, and you cannot make a strong beam by joining two trees together end to end. Ordinary houses were built in bays. The width of the bay was governed by the length of the tree available to span it; its height must also be that of the average tree. This imposed a natural limit on height and width, though of course you might join as many bays as you wished to the side or back of the first if you wanted to make the building wider or longer. It might be easier to do this with masonry pillars, and perhaps even with masonry arches; but even then the roof must be of wood.

In the eleventh century an "engineer" was an expert at designing siege engines, and there were no such people as architects. Normally the man who planned the construction of a great building described himself as a carpenter. He must do all his calculating in his head. Arabic figures were not yet known in the West, and Roman figures did not help him to add, subtract, or divide in writing. He might make a model of the effect he was aiming at, sometimes by drawing lines on a sand table, sometimes working in three dimensions with a lump of clay. That would be more to impress his patron than to help him solve a problem. He must carry in his head what weight or thrust would fall on each beam, and where the next beam would be needed. If he decided to play for safety his building would be wasteful of good timber; if he preferred to take a chance, his building might not stand up. Many large buildings of that time suffered from both defects; the first attempt collapsed before it was finished, and then it was built again with unnecessary weight and strength.

Once Harold has become a qualified carpenter he may be asked to design any kind of large timber building, from a banqueting hall to a barn. Wealthy burgesses of London will be eager to give a chance to the son of the well-known *butsecarle* Olaf. But if his early buildings fall down he will dwindle into a mere craftsman, fixing wooden shingles on a roof designed by another. Which kind of carpenter he becomes will depend on luck and his own self-confidence; there are no examinations for professional competence.

At ten years of age Robert is not too young to contribute to the support of his family. He helps in the stables of a big London inn, where he gets more in tips from satisfied merchants than in wages from the innkeeper.

Robert seems to have an affinity with mules and pack ponies. They stand quiet when he handles them, he can spot at once when they are sick or in pain, and sometimes the treatment he suggests does some good. He sees each of them as an individual, not just as another beast, and remembers them from previous journeys to London. It would be a pity to waste this natural talent. Robert wants to work with pack ponies for the rest of his life, and Olaf is quite willing that he should.

But Robert will not always be a mere hired groom, working for wages. One day he will inherit a respectable patrimony. As the youngest son he is Olaf's natural heir, according to the curious but ancient custom of borough-English. The theory behind it is that a burgess ought to support his youngest son by leaving him all his property, for the elder children will have learned a trade and be in a position to support themselves by the time their father dies. Eventually Olaf's little hoard of silver pennies will come to Robert. How much is in it not even Olaf knows, for to count this kind of nest egg is to incur bad luck. Some angel or demon, some supernatural being who dislikes avarice, will quickly take steps to impoverish any man who counts too carefully his reserve for a rainy day.

When this inheritance comes to Robert he will be able to buy a train of pack ponies, perhaps even a mule or two. Mules, who cannot breed, are scarce and more expensive than common ponies, though never so valuable as a big horse that can be ridden to war. In themselves, mules are more useful than ponies: so surefooted that they can carry a fragile load without breaking it, and a more comfortable ride for women and invalids and unwarlike clerks than the best-mannered horse. Of course an able-bodied man, a warrior, would be ashamed to be seen riding a mule.

Once Robert owns a string of ponies he will be able to hire them out to a merchant. He must hire out the whole string as a unit, for of course he will go with them to look after them. That means he will have to hire a few drivers to help him. These may be young Londoners starting to learn the trade, or they may be masterless outlanders of unknown origin. If they are to be safe in open country they ought to carry arms and know how to use them; so probably most of his unknown employees will be outlaws seeking a fresh start in life, or other fugitives from distant justice. At the outset Robert must get them to obey him by being even better armed and more warlike than they, and perhaps by judicious bluster. But very soon each man will develop a corporate loyalty to the pack train. After a year and a day, if he has maintained a home in London and not been absent from it too long, the outlander can claim to be a burgess protected by all the might of his city, which is a much better way of life than being a masterless outlaw. This influx of masterless men in search of protection was the main reason why the population of London continually increased, and presumably why the Londoners were so powerful in battle. But on his first journey Robert will be severely tested.

He must be willing to go anywhere within the Kingdom of England. If he is asked to cross the border into Wales or Scotland, that will be a matter of negotiation and extra pay. But within England he must go anywhere, and know the way. To know the way is fairly easy. The old Roman roads still radiate from London, they cannot be mistaken for byways, and they lead straight from one market town to the next. The older green roads first marked out by Bronze Age traders, the Icknield Way and others, are still in frequent use, especially by travelers from Wales or from oversea; but they were designed before London existed and ignore it, so they are not much use to a traveler starting from London.

Robert must be honest and trustworthy, and efficient at caring for pack animals. But if he is loyal to his employers, never yielding to the temptation to do a deal with a band of brigands, he ought to prosper. Under King William, the roads are safer than they have ever been before. The new Norman sheriffs, leading mounted men who can fight on horseback, usually break up any gang of outlaws within a few months. Then the outlaws will be blinded, so roughly that as a rule they die of it, which satisfies the letter of the law abolishing capital punishment, and at the same time rids the shire of troublesome criminals. But all the possessions of a felon are forfeit to the King, and from this source comes a substantial part of the royal income. As a rule a sheriff, who knows what the King expects from him, sends to the Treasury all the

property of every felon he catches; so that even if it was stolen from a merchant yesterday, and can still be easily identified, the merchant will never get it back.

The roads are safe, but once anything is stolen it is gone for good. A merchant cannot insure against being robbed, although insurance of that kind had existed in the days of the ancient Roman Empire. It is not that the idea of insurance has been forgotten. It is rather that everyone is always short of ready cash, since kings and barons hoard all they can, and that an insurance company which made a profit might be breaking the law against usury. Long-distance trade is a dangerous business, though it is richly rewarded if all goes well. No one expects that the improved safety of the roads will last; it so obviously depends on the forceful rule of King William, who will die one day. Robert will be earning his living at the risk of his life, just as his father did long ago on Viking cruise.

The future of the two boys is reasonably assured. Harold will be a skilled carpenter, with a chance to design his own buildings if he should prove capable of it. Robert will travel with pack ponies—his own ponies if he lays out his inheritance with prudence. If they turn out scatterbrained and foolish, they must work for others at a daily wage; but at least they will know how to do useful work, and richer men will be willing to hire them.

Matilda does not yet know what will become of her, though she also expects a prosperous future. In about three years' time, when her mother has taught her how to keep house, she will marry some burgess who will provide a home for her. Every householder needs a wife; if this wife should die he must immediately begin to look round for another. There are no elderly bachelors, and very few elderly widowers unless they have a daughter-in-law to look after them. With no flats to let, no lodging houses, no inns which offer permanent accommodations, a man must have a wife unless he is willing to do his own cooking and cleaning.

Matilda has greater freedom of choice than if she were a grand lady. If she falls in love with some young man who offers to marry her and can support her, Olaf will make no objection to a love match. If she has no particular views he will find a suitor for her, but he is content with the position he holds among the burgesses and is not looking for an influential son-in-law. All the same, she must soon begin to make up her mind. Her life as an attractive young girl will be very brief. Now that she is twelve, young men are already chaffing her in the street and making eyes at her in church on Sundays. If she is unmarried at sixteen, they will begin to think of her as an old maid. In a big town it is possible to live as an old maid by going out to work as an embroiderer or a seamstress, though weaving is considered man's work. But old maids are regarded as eccentric or unfortunate, and since they have no children to look after them in old age, they usually end as beggars at some church door.

Her great difficulty in making a choice is that she has so few opportunities to meet young men. No respectable young woman can be seen in a tavern, or in any of the walled enclosures where foreign merchants encamp. London has no night life. There are no theaters, no dance halls. On many religious holidays there are processions which end in public dancing. But all the elders are watching, and anyway the dances are very formal; there is never a chance for a young man to take a girl in his arms and whirl round with her.

All the same Matilda knows a lot about the young unmarried men of London, though more by hearsay than by direct conversation. The square mile of the city is divided into nearly a hundred parishes, so that on Sundays and great feasts practically all the burgesses go to Mass at about the same time of the day. A young girl, walking between her parents, may peep without seeming forward. She is welcome to watch the frequent musters of the militia; one reason why these parades are so popular is that they give the young men a chance to peacock in front of the girls. Most important of all, in the intense social life of the women, which scarcely touches the social life of the men, she often meets their sisters.

Probably she will wait until Olaf suggests a husband for her. Any man suggested by her father will be respectable and solvent, able and willing to support a wife. But if she does not care for her proposed partner she will put forward some other name, until in the end she and her parents are in agreement. Even in her social class, marriage is very seldom a private, personal affair; it is more of a formal alliance between two families.

Of course young people do occasionally elope; and if the stories told of those days are to be believed, the advances usually came from the girl rather than the young man. So long as they were properly married by a priest, nobody minded very strongly. But such a marriage, without dowry or portion, usually means a hard struggle for the young couple. Matilda is unlikely to fall in love so passionately that she will marry without the consent of her parents.

Soon after she is married, young children will begin to keep her at home, and when she does go out she must not look too attractive. She may look prosperous, if she can manage it; scarlet cloth trimmed with fur proves that her husband is doing well. But even rich gowns will not enhance her personal appearance. In the eleventh century clothes were never cut to fit the figure; they were meant to keep it out of sight. If a married woman were to try to look attractive everyone would be shocked.

She does not recognize that this is probably the happiest period of her life. She longs for the independent status of a wife and mother; when she has attained it she will sigh for the vanished freedom of her girlhood.

Shortly before midday Olaf comes home with a fine pork sausage, given to him by the master of a Baltic ship which made an unusually quick passage and has stores to spare. Emma grills it, and puts it on a mound of lettuce from the toft, which she has been boiling in water as we now boil cabbage. Everyone knows that raw greenstuff is dangerous to health, though no one has yet discovered why cooking it in boiling water makes it safe. Sausage, boiled lettuce, and plenty of fresh bread make a very good dinner for an ordinary weekday. The boys will dine with their masters.

Even in high summer they all begin work at dawn and continue until dark, so they can afford a long break for dinner at midday. They eat with wooden spoons from the iron cooking pot set on the floor between them. This is more convenient than it sounds, since they are also squatting on the floor. There are no benches in the house, and no chairs.

Before they begin Olaf mutters a form of Grace which has come down from his ancestors. He does not understand what he is saying, though he knows it is the appropriate thing to say. In fact the archaic Danish phrases are not unambiguously Christian; they would suit just as well an old-fashioned worshipper of Thor.

After they have eaten they recline on the floor for a full hour, sipping an occasional mouthful of ale and exchanging comments about the morning. Olaf has been repairing the standing rigging of a Rhineland ship. He will go back to the same job in the afternoon, though he does not expect to finish before tomorrow. Tonight he will be home before sunset, so that in the last of the light he can make fresh cord for the ratlines. He likes this German rig; it is very like Danish and not at all in the Norman fashion. But he cannot explain why he likes it, for he lacks words to make his meaning clear to females.

When Olaf has gone back to the German wharf, Emma and Matilda set out on a round of visits. There are no young babies in the house to keep them at home. Their first call is at the parish church, the natural meeting place of all the local wives. There Emma joins a group of her contemporaries, mothers and mothers-in-law who are free for the afternoon. They bring her up to date with all the births, marriages, and deaths in the district, and then all move off together for a round of sick-visiting.

Matilda has joined another group of girls. There is safety in numbers, and a dozen girls may walk the streets together without harm to anyone's reputation. They walk right across London from their riverside parish to the open fields north of the town. There they dance carols, round dances to which they sing their own accompaniment, until the sun is low and it is time to return home for supper. In the intervals between dances they gossip about their own families. It is very likely that Matilda's future husband is the brother of one of these girls, and when she marries him he will be surprised to discover how much she already knows about him.

The world of women is quite separate from the world of men. Wives do not often meet the husbands of their friends, just as men seldom meet the wives of other men. But gossip is the chief amusement of Londoners of both sexes, so that everyone soon learns of the doings of all the neighbors.

At his stables, Robert is busy until full dark. A train of pack ponies came in from the west just before dinner-time, and another in the afternoon. He has to unload them, feed them, and rub them down. Harold finishes early, before sunset. He has just planed and smoothed a big plank, and it does not seem worth while to begin another task before tomorrow.

In the workshops of London no one tears into his work until he puffs and sweats; the hours are too long for that sort of exertion. But everyone keeps at it steadily, without coffee breaks. Workmen cannot watch the clock because there is never a clock within view. They gossip all the time, but their hands move as they talk and they are never completely idle. By the end of the day they have got through a great deal, and they are not especially tired.

Harold, who stopped early and has a farthing to spare, goes to a tavern until supper shall be ready. The enormous wooden pot of ale he gets for his money is enough to keep him busy until dark. He overhears the conversation of some traveling merchants who are discussing the state of the road to Southampton and the chances of being robbed on it. He has nothing to contribute, but what he hears may be useful to Robert. There are no newspapers from which to learn the condition of the roads.

Olaf, of course, has been discussing world politics and his own travels in foreign countries since first he went on board this German ship. News from all Christendom comes to London, and it can come only by word of mouth. Conversation is regarded as an art; people in general take pride in telling a good story, and most stories are improved in the telling. The long hours of work never seem dull.

During the summer there are no holidays. The longest holiday comes in midwinter, when the Twelve Days of Christmas may be spent by the fireside or in a warm, crowded church. On Sundays no one is supposed to work for his living, though of course animals must be tended and meals cooked. This Sunday rest is enforced by a law of the Church, backed by the commands of the King and the custom of the local community. It is hard to say exactly what would happen to anyone who openly defied this law, though we can gather from ancient sermons that the avaricious sometimes tried to break it by stealth. The law against Sunday work was especially irksome to those dependent on the weather; a fine day wasted after a succession of storms would be hard on a fisherman, a good head of water after a long drought would tempt a miller. In the sermons these wicked fishermen and millers are punished by the direct intervention of Heaven. Such stories never deal with a craftsman living in a crowded town, so presumably no burgess dared to defy public opinion as a lonely countryman might. Besides Sundays there are holidays of obligation, when every Christian, after hearing Mass in the morning, may spend the rest of the day in recreation. These holiday afternoons can be the occasion for a muster of the militia, which will end in a jolly drinking party.

On six days of the week Olaf and his sons expect to work from dawn to sunset. Their main amusement is talk, which can be combined with work. When they are not working, the drinking of ale is their chief recreation. As for personal dignity, they are members of the "great and terrible army of London," which bargained as an equal with King William, which in the next century will place King Stephen on the throne and keep him there.

Emma and Matilda lead their own busy lives, parallel with but seldom touching that of the men. They cannot fight, and therefore the law grants them few rights. But the Church stands ready to protect them as wives and mothers. Under Christian monogamy they are infinitely better off than were the women of pagan Greece or Rome.

Cosmopolitan London has taken the Norman Conquest in its stride. Every year it grows bigger and more prosperous. Among the burgesses there is no racial prejudice, as we can see from the extraordinary mixture of names they give to their sons. The sum of the taxes they owe to the King has been settled firmly; no Norman baron dares to blackmail them. King William is stern and quick to punish, but a powerful ruler is good for trade. Few of the old men regret the cheerful and lawless days of good King Edward.

IV · THE CHILDREN
OF THE CLOISTER

During the persecutions of Diocletian towards the end of the third century, Saint Alban was martyred outside the Roman city of Verulamium. His fellow Christians have never forgotten him, or the site of his martyrdom. About the time of the Saxon invasion of Britain, the town of Verulamium fell into complete ruin, but as soon as the English had become Christian an English king, Offa, founded a great monastery on a hill outside its walls, the traditional place of the martyrdom. Between the days of the Heptarchy and 1087, the Abbey of St. Albans had its ups and downs. Under stress of the Danish invasions, the monks were replaced by secular canons.

Saint Dunstan brought back the Benedictine Rule. Now, during the last year of the reign of King William the Conqueror, the monastery is beginning a long period of greatness and prosperity.

It is not one of the wealthiest abbeys in England. The Domesday commissioners reckoned its income at £270 when Glastonbury had £830. But its site gives it several advantages. Most of the abbey lands lie close beside it, within a block of territory marked out in the tenth century by four churches. That makes it much easier to administer than, say, the lands of Westminster, which lie scattered all over England. The abbey itself stands just beside Watling Street, the old Roman road from London to Chester. It is within an easy day's ride of London, so that it receives a constant stream of distinguished visitors who can tell the monks all the news of England and Normandy. Those who leave London for the north or west spend the first night of their journey in the guest house. At the foot of the hill lie the ruins of Verulamium, a useful quarry for building materials. Best of all, on the hilltop outside the enclosure a considerable town is growing up, inhabited by craftsmen and traders dependent on the abbey. Because they dwell on abbey land the abbot is in every sense their lord, according to the established feudal theory of the day. If they break the law and are compelled to pay for it, the money goes to Saint Alban, not to the King. Even if they keep the law they must pay something, since burgesses cannot render labor service; for their houses and shops they must pay rent in silver.

Thus a large proportion of the abbey's revenue is paid in cash, which may be collected very easily. From their agricultural estates the monks draw more in produce than they can consume, and the town is an excellent market in which to sell the surplus. Respectable guests always leave a thank-offering after receiving hospitality from the abbey. In fact Saint Alban can usually lay his hands, or the hands of his deputy, on ready money, which is more than can always be said of the King.

Saint Alban, of course, has been dead for many centuries, but he is still in a very real sense the lord of his abbey. His body lies actually within the abbey church, and in Heaven he can see all that passes on earth. No prudent burgess of his town, no farmer of his lands, would dare to brave the wrath of Saint Alban. Even those who do not always act honestly will fear to cheat the saint, or his monks.

The visible head of the community, the deputy of Saint Alban, is the abbot; and since this is a particular monastery at a particular period, something can be said about the actual abbots, past and present. (Monasteries varied so much in their circumstances and their manner of facing the secular world that it is impossible to discuss an average community.)

According to the Rule composed by Saint Benedict, an abbot should be chosen by his monks in free election. But then in the early Church, bishops—at least some bishops —were elected by a mass meeting of all the Christians in the diocese. By the eleventh century, free election to any post, clerical or lay, was a rare occurrence within the Kingdom of England, which cannot be described at that time as a democracy.

This is what we know about the eleventh-century abbots of St. Albans. In 1066 the abbot was one Fritheric, a member of the Danish royal house related to King Canute. Presumably he had been recommended by some Danish prince, or by the great Earl Godwin (the father of King Harold), who favored the Danish party; though before he was installed in office he must have been elected by the monks, or by a deputation chosen from the monks. The form of election was still necessary. Monks, like English country freeholders in the later Middle Ages, did not care to choose sides and stand up to be counted, presumably because they did not wish to go on record, for what might be a long abbatial reign, as having supported the defeated candidate. If some community was so poor and unimportant, or the King so lacking in interest, that its members were permitted a free and unfettered election, they often appointed a committee of about a dozen monks who picked an abbot after secret deliberations. But a community was just as likely to elect the monk of highest birth they could find. A Danish prince may have been elected quite freely, because he would not be afraid to stand up to a bishop or even a king. Fritheric may have been the unanimous choice of the community.

This Danish abbot did not appreciate the Norman Conquest. In 1070 he ran off to Ely to join Hereward and his band of rebels. In due course he was declared an outlaw, and the abbey was considered vacant. By this time King William had got rid of Stigand, the uncanonical Danish Archbishop of Canterbury. To succeed him he appointed Lanfranc, Abbot of the Norman abbey of Caen.

Though Lanfranc came to England from a Norman monastery, he was not a Norman. He had been born in northern Italy, and had won fame as a teacher of canon law before he entered the poorest and most squalid monastery he could find in all Normandy. As a monk he was persuaded to continue with his lectures, and at once Bec became famous as the best school and most holy community in northern France. King William took him from this monastery, where he was prior, and made him, first, Abbot of Caen and then Archbishop of Canterbury.

Lanfranc was already so famous for learning and holiness that he governed the Church in England more as though he were a local pope than an archbishop. St. Albans lay within the diocese of Lincoln, and it owed the service of six knights to the King. But without consulting either the Bishop of Lincoln or the King, Lanfranc appointed a monk from Normandy to be abbot. Abbot Paul, though he came from a Norman monastery, was by birth another north Italian, and Lanfranc's nephew. But no one whispered of nepotism; Abbot Paul was so obviously the right man for the job. In 1087 he was still ruling St. Albans and had made it one of the most important monasteries in England.

Monks are rather a special kind of people, who do not fit easily into any legal system. They cannot marry, they cannot hold property, they must obey their abbot in everything, and they have sworn never to leave the monastery of their choice. King William's lawyers deal with this by pretending that when a man is professed a monk he counts as dead. He cannot inherit property, he cannot be a suitor in any court, he cannot be called on for military service. As regards property, the next heir inherits, just as if the monk were really dead. The law has not yet decided what to do if he holds land when he becomes a monk. Sometimes his land goes to his abbey, sometimes to his heir by blood. But not many monks hold land when they take their vows, for most of them enter the monastery as children.

To us nowadays that must seem an astonishing state of affairs. A monk's vocation is an unusual one. In the modern world it is carefully tested during a long novitiate, and a large proportion of novices do not persevere to final profession. In the eleventh century most monks began their training about the age of seven, because their parents had commanded them to enter the religious life.

The analogy is with baptismal vows. If a baby in arms can undertake by proxy all the obligations of a Christian, then why cannot a father promise that his son will become a monk? Furthermore, it does in fact work. Most of "the children of the cloister," as they are called, in due time become satisfactory monks.

By the eleventh century the full rigors of the system have been alleviated. There had been a time when a boy who entered the cloister made his full profession on admittance; if in later life he went out into the world, he would be in mortal sin, excommunicate, and incidentally an outlaw. If a sheriff caught such a runaway it was his duty to return him to his abbot.

Now, under King William, all the children of the cloister rank as novices. No one is permitted to make his full profession until he is "adolescent," some time between the ages of sixteen and twenty-one. But there is, as there always has been, another source of recruits. A grown man may become a monk at any age. Herluin, the founder of Bec and Lanfranc's abbot, was a knight more than thirty years old when he left the world. Reinfrid, a knight who had helped to conquer England, went off in middle age to refound Whitby. Anketil, already a skilled goldsmith, in the twelfth century entered St. Albans and designed a splendid new shrine for the tomb of the martyr.

But these late vocations could not join in the full life of the community. A choirmonk must be able to read fluently, and to sing as he reads; the Office and psalms, on which he spends most of his time, vary daily throughout the liturgical year. Constant repetition gives the average monk a good memory, perhaps because he has so few outside distractions. But those who knew the full psalter by heart were exceptional; and one abbot who could repeat every psalm backwards, verse by verse, was held to be unique.

Not very many laymen can read fluently, and it is taken for granted that most of them will be unable to learn in middle life. Charlemagne, with a mind a good deal better than average, tried to learn how to read after he was King of the Franks, and never succeeded though he spent many hours at it. But any child can be taught to read, if there is someone to teach him.

That is why the children of the cloister are such an important source of recruitment. Most of the monks of St. Albans have been about the place since they were very small. As a matter of fact the abbey, which takes a keen interest in education, maintains another school. But the grammar school in the town, though it attracts the sons of wealthy men from all over England, has nothing but a financial connection with the abbey. The master—there is only one master—is appointed by the abbot and presumably paid from monastic revenues; but he is a secular clerk, not a monk, and does not commonly visit the monastery.

The children of the cloister, on the other hand, live most of the time within the enclosure; though since they are not yet professed monks they are free to go outside on certain days. They also have only one master, who comes fairly low in the monastic hierarchy; that is to say, we sometimes learn incidentally that a particular monk has been master of the children, though in the formal account of his rise from choirmonk to abbot such an appointment is not considered worth mention.

In this chapter we shall examine the lives of three children who are being taught in the cloister school of St. Albans in July 1087. Richard is the son of a Norman baron, who was once in a tight place from which he did not expect to escape alive; he vowed that if he lived to see another son born to him he would devote him to

God. Henry had a Breton father and an English mother, though at home they spoke more French than English. Ethelwulf, as his name implies, comes from an English family of noble birth. It is perhaps worth pointing out that most monks come from fairly prosperous families, not because monasteries are snobbish or demand an entrance fee, but because poor parents cannot afford to forgo the labor of a son who may help to support them in old age. Two of these boys come from French-speaking homes and one from an English-speaking one, but that hardly matters. Only very young new arrivals are allowed to speak any language other than Latin.

Like everyone else in a well-run monastery, the children of St. Albans are always short of sleep. Lying asleep in bed, as opposed to nodding on a seat during the afternoon, is regarded as a slothful indulgence and a potential occasion of sin. Though some satirists, especially in England, have accused Benedictine monks of eating too much, no one has ever accused them of late rising. The daily Office, in the great abbey-church, begins at 2:00 at the latest. Choirmonks can get up quickly, for they sleep in their clothes and do not wash until just before dinner. The children, who are not yet monks, come into church rather later. But they remain through the long service, mainly of chanted psalms, which continues without a break until about 6:00. Of course, no one has yet eaten anything.

We know in some detail what monks did every day at this period, because Archbishop Lanfranc himself laid down a timetable for them. It is not very easy to follow this timetable, since it takes little account of the clock. It lays down that this must follow that, with no estimate of how long each part of the program will endure—except for vague references to the rising of the sun that may follow without alteration the time of the sunrise in the latitude of Rome. After this long morning service, the children are not mentioned. We know that they ate breakfast while the monks were still fasting, and that they would not be allowed to attend Chapter, the daily business meeting. That was for monks only, and met some time soon after 6:00 A.M.

No monk would eat before midday, but there was a special breakfast of bread and milk for the children. That is certainly true of St. Albans, for a particular endowment had been given to pay for it. When the monks came out of church at about six, they put on their day shoes. Hitherto they had been wearing slippers, the only difference between their day and night attire. They washed, and combed their hair. Presumably about the same time, the children washed and ate their breakfast.

About 8:00 came the main religious event of the day, the sung High Mass. We know that the children were there, or some of them, since the music was arranged for treble voices as well as for the double choir of monks. That would be finished about 9:30 and presumably the children then began their schooling for the day.

At midday came dinner, when the monks first tasted food, about ten hours after they had risen from their beds. Meat is never permitted within the refectory, though because of the accident that Saint Benedict wrote "quad-

ruped" when he meant "animal," chickens and other birds may be served. So the children have a separate dining room: we know for certain that they might eat meat except on days of abstinence. The literal-minded monks of the eleventh century have decided that meat will defile the refectory, not the digestion of a monk. If the master of the children dines with his charges, or if some other monk happens to be traveling abroad on the business of his abbey, he may take what is put before him. In the same way, the sick who dine in the infirmary may eat anything that will do them good—though they must not prescribe for themselves, but take what is put before them.

After dinner comes a siesta, which helps to make up for very early rising. At 2:30 there are a few prayers in church, and then the monks work in the cloister from 3:00 to 5:30. In the summer only, they eat a light supper, then back to church again until bedtime about 8:00 P.M. That will give them a little less than six hours sleep, until the next day begins about 2:00 in the morning.

This would be on an average weekday in July, a month when there are few important feasts or fasts. It adds up to a long religious service in church from 2:00 A.M. to 9:30 A.M., an afternoon of mingled prayer and work—all sedentary work, naturally—one square meal and a snack every day, and a very early bedtime. In winter, which is chiefly made up of the penitential seasons of Advent and Lent, there is no supper, though in recompense they get up a little later. On great feasts there is, of course, no work, but the service in church lasts much longer. Besides the normal feasts of the Universal Church, each monastery has its own peculiar calendar to commemorate past abbots and benefactors. There is a natural tendency to elaborate great feasts by adding more lessons and more chants; until at Cluny in particular, the French abbey which was famous for the splendor of its ceremonial, visitors complained that a really great feast could not be finished within twenty-four hours. It must therefore encroach on the vigil of the day before or on the ordinary weekday which followed.

But if we look more closely we discover that, although all this took place as ordained, not every monk attended every service in church from start to finish. The abbot is a great lord, commander of a contingent of knights and by right a member of the King's Great Council. At this period he still lives with his monks when he is at home; but he is frequently away on secular business. Even when he is in the abbey he must often be writing letters while the other monks are in choir. The cellarer, business manager of all the abbey's revenues, must spend a great deal of his time on his accounts and on interviewing complaining tenants; he may have to go away to look into an unsatisfactory estate. Someone will have to look after the lay guests. The master of the children must have time for his lessons. During the next century the number of monks employed on special tasks, and so excused regular attendance in choir, increased until sometimes half the monks in any house had some form of special exemption. Then the choirmonks, "who bore the burden and heat of the day," came to be regarded as a kind of rank and file, waiting to be promoted to some more interesting work, pitied and despised by busy functionaries.

But this abuse still lies in the future. Under Abbot Paul the only "obedientiaries" of St. Albans, compelled by Holy Obedience to put their special responsibilities before the Divine Office, are the prior, the second in command; the cellarer, the business manager; the precentor, in charge of the liturgical furnishing of the church and of all the candles, oils, and other accessories; and the cantor, who manages the music.

These officials are appointed by the abbot, and in a sense share some of his absolute power. Even in 1087 there must have been other specialists, though we do not hear of them until later. The infirmarian, whose duty it was to care for sick monks, cannot have spent every morning in choir. There were two guardians of the shrine, who watched in turn, day and night, to see that no pilgrim stole a relic from the tomb of Saint Alban; they must have had some time in bed, even though monks manage with very little sleep.

During the long reign of Abbot Paul the monks of St. Albans increased in numbers from about fifty to a hundred. If in 1087, after Paul had been abbot for more than sixteen years, they numbered about seventy-five, probably about sixty would be regularly present in choir.

We know for certain that the children came into church after the very early morning Office had begun, because Lanfranc's Statutes allow for a pause while they catch up by saying what the monks have already sung. It is not quite certain that they stayed to the end;

perhaps they went back to bed for an hour or two. We know also that they were present at the sung High Mass. We do not know exactly how their days were occupied otherwise, but we know what they were supposed to have learned by the time they took their final vows.

The chief duty of a monk is, and always has been, to sing the Divine Office. According to the Rule of Saint Benedict he ought also to do some work on every day on which work is permissible: that is, on every day which is not a Sunday or a feast. In very early times monks worked on the land, though if they were to pass at least eight hours a day in choir they could not in addition support themselves entirely by agriculture. But by the eleventh century, monks no longer do manual work. They are supported from the estates given to them by pious benefactors. But they need more than food, clothes, and lodging; they need a great many service books, at least one to be shared between every two monks in choir. During most of their working time they copy and repair these much-handled service books before they wear out.

But since all monks can read and write, while very few laymen are literate, there is other writing for them to do. Most monasteries keep a chronicle, a diary of important events as they take place; and St. Albans in particular specializes in composing elaborate histories. In addition, the work of the past must be preserved, the best classical authors as examples of how Latin should be written. All our present-day versions of classical authors stem from manuscripts copied by monks; none have come down from the periods when they were first written. Monks multiply copies of works of Christian theology; in fact, since they borrow books from other monasteries and then copy them, the library of every monastery soon becomes very like the library of every other. Some monks, presumably with leave from the abbot, compose original work. Most Bibles are copied in monasteries. That must have been a terrifying undertaking. We of the present day are so accustomed to handling Bibles which have been printed and bound that we can hardly imagine the feelings of a monk who copies the first verse of Genesis and intends to go on to the end of Revelations. It is a task that will endure for life.

Every choirmonk has been taught to write in the same clear, regular hand, as easy to read as print. It is impossible to distinguish between the individual handwriting of different monks of the eleventh century. In a few East Anglian monasteries, self-consciously English and hostile to Norman intruders, they still write English in a separate form of lettering—quite reasonably, since English has a few letters which do not appear in the normal Latin alphabet. But St. Albans, ruled by a Norman abbot, in close touch with Canterbury and a day's journey from the royal abbey of Westminster, writes only in Latin.

Rough notes and ephemeral messages may be scribbled on smooth tablets of beechwood. But an enduring book must be written on clean parchment, with a well-cut pen, in ink which will last. During the eleventh century these things can seldom be bought in a shop, and no monastery likes to buy things which can be made at home. To smooth parchment, to cut pens, and to mix ink are the chief duties of the senior children of the cloister.

When the monks come out from Chapter, the daily business meeting where financial matters are decided, defaulters reproved, and the corporate seal of the abbey affixed to legal documents, they go straight to their desks in the cloister and expect to find everything ready for them. They are eager to begin, because most of them enjoy their work; and also because while working they are permitted to talk to one another. In the church they must sing the chant, at dinner they must listen in silence while someone reads aloud from a suitable book; in the cloister private conversation is allowed—of course, in Latin only. They work in short, broken periods, from 7:30 to 8:00, from 9:30 to 11:30, from 3:00 P.M. to 5:30. At the summons of the church bell they must drop whatever they are doing and come instantly. So their desks are left undisturbed and untidied all day. In the evening the senior children clear up after them and put everything away neatly, as they put it out in the morning.

On Sundays and other great feasts the monks do no writing or reading, for these tasks count as servile work. They pass a very much longer time in church, they eat a better dinner, and perhaps they have a longer siesta in the afternoon. We may be sure that they never have any time to spare, for all surviving accounts of what monks did every day in the eleventh century seem to fit more into the day than can be accomplished in twenty-four hours. But, presumably, teaching in school was reckoned just as much servile work as composing a history, so the master of the children would be busy in choir, and no desks need to be set up and tidied away in the cloister. After a good deal of attendance in church, the children would have a few hours of holiday.

How long they spend in school on other days it is impossible to say. By the time their schooldays are finished they will have been taught a good deal, but then they never went home to their parents.

To begin with they have to learn Latin, so thoroughly that they can speak and think in it as well as in their mother tongue, whatever that may have been. What they speak is not exactly classical Latin as Cicero spoke it, but it is grammatically correct. It employs a very wide vocabulary, with a great many words borrowed from Greek. It can be very rhetorical and diffuse, though the preferred models are the simple sentences used by Saint Jerome in the Vulgate. Considering that at this period no one speaks Latin from infancy, it is astonishing how familiar it becomes to clerks. In the twelfth century a grammatical howler uttered by the Bishop of Chichester in a speech to the Pope had all the college of cardinals roaring with laughter immediately, though they could not have been expecting it. Clerks, though not as a rule monks, are fond of making puns and jingles and remarks with a broad double meaning. Apparently no clerk ever had to search in his mind for the right Latin word, or had any difficulty putting into Latin, as fast as he heard them, speeches delivered in French or English. In the eleventh century the educated clergy spoke Latin as fluently as if they had been ancient Romans.

For beginners there were books on grammar, full of elaborate rules. But since all these books were themselves written in Latin, some proficiency would be required before embarking on them. When the children first entered the cloister they must have begun to speak Latin as a baby learns to speak his mother tongue, just by hearing it spoken round him.

At the same time they must learn to read, but in the eleventh century no one considered that very difficult. Just as it was assumed that no adult could ever learn his letters, so it was assumed that any boy, if taken young enough, could manage it. Reading is not, in fact, a very difficult operation.

It is much more difficult to learn how to write, though it is genuinely easier for young boys than for adults. A child's hands can be trained, while those of an adult are set in their habits. At the present day there are children who can write before they have learned to pick their way among the massed knives and forks of a formal dinner. There is no record of a child of the cloister who failed to learn reading and writing, after even a brief stay in a monastery.

A monk must be able to write well, but there is no need for him to write speedily. In some cases it is the custom to rule lines faintly on the page; after the book is finished these pencil marks may be erased. He will write his letters very large, so that they may be read by a stranger standing at a lectern, without glasses; and he may let himself go with the decoration. Every capital letter, written even larger than the rest, may be embellished with at least a pen-and-ink sketch. If it is to be painted in several colors, the writer will indicate a simple outline in faint pencil and then turn it over to the miniature-painter.

The object is to produce a beautiful book, easy to read and pleasant to handle. The miniatures and other decorations on every page will give a stranger some indication of the portion of text before him, much as running page headings do nowadays. If to write even a short treatise in this fashion takes a very long time, well, no monk ought to be in a hurry and the delay will be an excellent preparation for eternity.

Abbot Paul, we happen to know, was eager to increase the library of his abbey. Perhaps he had been shocked by a dearth of service books when he took over. Even the large number of monks at his command worked too slowly. He took the unusual step—unusual for the eleventh century though it became more common later—of hiring lay scribes and setting aside a room in the monastery for them to work in. Of course they had a room of their own; no abbot would like to have laymen working beside his monks in the cloister and distracting them with gossip from the secular world.

During the periods of work a monk may read as well as write, presumably with permission from the abbot. A monk who is to compose an original work needs all the education he can get. He ought to have read all the classical authors in the monastic library, so that his Latin will be elegant and correct. But since these authors were pagans, he need not read them more than once. After that he can go on quoting phrases from them as though he knew them by heart; for as he reads he compiles a notebook of elegant extracts, such as striking phrases to describe a very wicked man or, more rarely, a very good man. He may be lucky enough to come by a book of quotations put together by some monk now dead, and then he will be able to quote from authors he has never read.

One reason monastic chroniclers give such a gloomy description of the world around them is that the classics available in the library were mostly the work of satirists. It is fairly easy to lift from them a biting phrase of condemnation, not so easy to find words of praise.

In addition, a monk with any literary ambitions ought to keep up with current theology and political theory by reading new books as soon as they arrive in the monastery. All this has to be done in not more than five hours of a long day, by a sleepy man whose main task is to chant the Office. When we remember the timetable by which monks lived, it is astonishing that they produced any new literature at all.

The children of the cloister seem to have mastered all these subjects—Latin, reading, writing—without any difficulty. What does seem to have bothered them was finding the correct Latin word for the ordinary small affairs of daily life. The only schoolbooks that have come down to us from the eleventh century are dialogues between master and pupil, obviously composed to give the boy a wide Latin vocabulary covering the events of every day.

From these we learn something of the daily life of such boys. It seems that they ate well, even though not very often. They might eat meat, since they were not as yet bound by any vows. Oddly enough, they seem to have possessed a little pocket money, perhaps sent them by their parents. In one of these dialogues the master asks the boy what he drinks with his meals. The answer is beer when he can get it, otherwise water; wine is too expensive, and too strong to be drunk by children. This seems to imply that the boys might sometimes buy beer.

The master must have been teaching in the schoolroom while the other monks were in church. A reasonable guess at the timetable is that the children passed most of the morning in church, with a short break while they ate breakfast and arranged the writing desks of the monks. About 9:30 they would start their schooling, after the monks had finished the sung High Mass and gone to their desks. They would continue until dinner at midday. After the siesta they would go into school again at about 2:30, and keep at it until supper at 5:30.

On an ordinary weekday this leaves no time for recreation. But we know that the boys sometimes went on rambles in the country, for they were not yet monks who might not leave the enclosure without permission. These outings could take place on Sundays and other feasts, when the master might not work and therefore there could food, drink, and what they would see on these outings, as be no school. The surviving dialogues treat largely of a means of teaching them the Latin names for everyday things. A senior schoolboy might be able to read advanced theology and the poems of Persius, the Roman satirist, and still not know the correct Latin for beer and cheese and the various works of husbandry, because such things are not mentioned by serious authors.

Let us look at the children more closely, as they eat their dinner on a weekday in July 1087. They have a dining room of their own, within the enclosure so that the master can supervise them without seeking an obedience from the abbot to go outside. But the room is quite separate from the monks' refectory, for on the table are roast mutton and boiled bacon. About forty boys, aged between seven and sixteen, sit on both sides of the table on long benches; the schoolmaster sits at the head of it, on a stool.

At first glance the boys look like miniature monks. They wear long black gowns reaching to the ankle and low shoes on their stockingless feet. Their heads are closely cropped; a short fuzz on the crown proves that they are tonsured clerks, though the tonsure was last renewed some weeks ago. But anyone who understands clerical dress can see that they are not monks. Their black gowns are not the wide cowls, with hood attached, which form the full costume of a Benedictine choirmonk. At his girdle each boy carries a wallet in which he may store his personal possessions; he is not yet vowed to poverty.

Dinner is the only square meal of the day, so there is a great deal of food on the table. Besides dishes of mutton and bacon, both much cheaper fare than the roast beef of the well-to-do, there are salads, bowls of beans and bowls of porridge, and loaves of every kind of bread. With their bread they may eat butter, lard, or honey, as they wish. There may also be a bowl of fish, smothered in a savory sauce: a specialty of St. Albans known to us from a characteristic anecdote.

When Abbot Paul arrived in 1070 he found, to his horror, that the English monks ate meat from time to time, presumably to celebrate great feasts. They explained that this had been the custom of the house since time immemorial, but of course it was clean contrary to the Rule. The Norman-Italian abbot did not rely on his authority, either as a religious superior or as a representative of the conquering race. He was determined not to rival the scandalous behavior of the Norman Abbot Thurstan at Glastonbury. In that holy and venerable abbey there arose a difference of opinion about how to sing the chant, a matter on which monastic opinion may be strongly aroused at the present day. After a stormy meeting in Chapter, this came to a pitched battle within the church. The English monks barricaded themselves in the choir; the abbot called out his Norman bodyguard, armed with spears and bows. When the monks tried to defend the choir screen by using candlesticks as clubs, the archers began to shoot. In the end the monks were driven from the choir, with three killed and many wounded. As soon as King William heard of it, Thurstan was exiled in disgrace.

Abbot Paul was more forbearing. Instead of using arrows, he brought over a French cook. Fish cooked in the

French manner proved more appetizing than English roast beef, and the monks of their own volition went back to the diet ordained by Saint Benedict. The masterpiece of this cook was a pie filled with carp; but we must remember that the tastes of our ancestors were not at all the same as ours.

Abbot Paul's cook is not a monk. By the eleventh century Benedictine monks are too busy in church and cloister to do their own housekeeping. They maintain a great many servants to cook, to clean, to wash up. A monk is, among other things, a scholar who expects to be waited on. His life is certainly not idle, but he has no time to sweep his own floors. At St. Albans the servants, all male so that they may live within the enclosure, slightly outnumber the monks they serve.

Thus the children of the cloister find their table laid for them, and may leave it in disorder. A boy arranges the writing desks of the choirmonks rather to teach him humility than because there is no one else to do it.

At fifteen Richard is one of the senior boys, expected to keep an eye on the conduct of his juniors. If he sees anyone behaving badly, he will report the culprit to the master without hesitation: in religious foundations there has never been any prejudice against tale-bearing. Anyone he reports will be beaten; but then he also will be beaten for any slight fault, and so indeed for that matter might an adult choirmonk. In a monastery a keen sense of personal dignity is obviously out of place, and in a monastery of the eleventh century a flogging may happen to anyone. The master of the children has been chosen for his rather lowly task because, among other qualifications, he can wield the rod with vigor.

During the eight years he has been at St. Albans, Richard has become well adjusted to the religious life. All around him are boys who look forward to their profession, or monks who are still thankful that they have chosen the better part. His father, when he brought him to the monastery, promised him that after some discomfort in this world he will inherit eternal life, and Richard has never doubted the truth of that promise. Of course, he is careful to remember that he is a sinful man who must strive constantly, but there are plenty of people all round him eager to point out his personal failings. What troubles him most is that so often he feels radiantly happy in what is designed to be a penitential way of life. A good monk may feel an inner serenity, but he ought not to go about grinning from ear to ear.

Richard, descended from successful Norman knights, has inherited their energy and self-control. He is intelligent enough to see in his mind's eye the ideal community which Abbot Paul is trying to bring down from Heaven to St. Albans. At this dinner he heaps his wooden bowl with porridge, for he never eats meat unless some superior orders him to do so to keep up his strength. He is thinking how much more enjoyable is his life than if he had remained in the world.

He dislikes getting up in the middle of the night; he is quite sure he will never get used to it, if he should live for forty years as a monk. But then it is not meant to be pleasant, so he is fulfilling the wish of Saint Benedict when he jumps out of bed sleepy and shivering with cold. But once he gets into church, happiness returns. The chant must be very like what the angels sing eternally in Heaven. His own voice is breaking, so he can take no part in it; but when he could sing treble he used to add his share, and when he is a grown man and professed it will be the chief occupation of his life. He is beginning to recognize subtle shades of meaning in all the Latin psalms. Every time he hears them repeated he discovers new depths in them. Just to sing the psalms all day is the best occupation for any man. It will be his occupation, thanks to the generous benefactors of the past who have provided this splendid abbey for him. He remembers them with fervor during the prayers for the dead, and also during the extra prayers for the royal family of England which are a special feature of the ritual of St. Albans. Indeed, if King William is the rightful successor to King Edward, as all good Normans believe, and if King Edward was the rightful successor to the ancient King Offa of Mercia, then past benefactors and the present royal house are much the same group.

The peak of his day is the sung High Mass soon after 8:00 A.M. Richard often misses his breakfast so that he may receive Communion then, instead of at the earlier spoken Morrow Mass before Chapter. Some day, years hence, he may himself be ordained priest; but he is sure that even then he will seldom offer a private Mass. Spiritually, it is more satisfying, it will always be more satisfying, to share this great happiness with the other brethren of the community.

Richard is also entranced by his discovery of Latin literature. The French he spoke as a child is still regarded as a degenerate and ungrammatical form of Latin. It has no fixed spelling, because no one writes seriously in it. Since it is at bottom a form of slang, it changes and goes out of date with great rapidity. How much better to learn the correct—that is, the Latin—way of speaking.

In Latin you may tell of a great event, or describe the character of an eminent man, in language that will never alter. You may write it down so that future ages will share exactly in your thought. The ancient Romans told stories superbly, for all that they were ignorant pagans, and you may still enter into their feelings. To speak Latin, to read and write Latin until you think in that language and no other, is one of the great privileges of the religious life.

Richard never wishes to leave the enclosure. The periods he likes least in his schooldays are the afternoons of great feasts, when after a morning in church the boys go off together into the open country. On these afternoons he is often shocked by the goings-on of his companions. They steal apples off the trees, for every child of the eleventh century felt an unsatisfied craving for fresh fruit. They break down hedges. If the boys of the town throw stones at them, they sometimes pick up the stones and throw them straight back. It is all very shocking.

Richard does his best to restrain these riotous companions. First he gives them fair warning; then, if they do not behave themselves, he tells the master of the children all about their crimes and sins. Or rather, he used to do that until a few weeks ago. Then, while Richard was putting out the desks in the cloister, the abbot himself spoke to him. The abbot is not bound by any timetable, and you may run into him at any moment; though never before had he gone out of his way to speak to Richard, who was thrilled by the honor.

But what Abbot Paul said was neither thrilling nor honorable. He reminded the boy that he is still in strict theory a layman, or at most a tonsured clerk. So are all the other boys in the school. They are not compelled to behave like monks, especially when they are well away from the abbey. If Richard sees them do anything that would be sinful if done by a layman it is his duty to report it; but if he sees them merely behave in a manner unfitting to monks, he must remember that they are not professed.

Since then Richard has reported no misdemeanors.

Perhaps a boy like Richard sounds too good to be true, or possibly too priggish, but monastic records are full of people like that. Our own posterity may not be able to imagine that anyone could live under the discipline of a regular soldier's life in peacetime, but we all know that it can easily be endured. So it was with the monks of the eleventh century. In some ways their spiritual life was narrow. They never wished to meditate, or to speak directly to God in their own words. What they liked was to read psalms, or to repeat them by rote, and the more of that they did every day the happier they were.

Henry is also reasonably happy in the life that has been chosen for him, though he is not happy for the same reasons as Richard. The long mornings in church bore him. His voice is rough; the cantor encourages him to keep it low, which suits him well. If the master of the children is busy or sick, and excused from attendance in choir, Henry will sometimes try to doze through the long Office. In his heart he does not believe that the correct chant is the most important aspect of the religious life— an opinion that he would never dare to voice to the other children. As for the professed choirmonks, he never has an opportunity to speak to them anyway. He longs for his bed, and even more for his dinner. His faith, of course, is absolutely firm. In eleventh-century England there were no unbelievers. He knows that to praise God is the main duty in life, and that he ought to think himself lucky to spend so many hours at it every day. But he does not really come alive until he sits down at his desk.

Then the whole world lies open before him: all its history, all the daring thoughts of the pagan philosophers of old, all the even more daring speculations of modern theologians. For full measure, there are also the travelers' tales which make up geography, and the windy theorizing of political idealists.

At home Henry's father spoke Breton and French, his mother English. He grew up knowing bits of three languages, so that Latin came easily to him. Learning to read was not so easy, but he is neat with his hands and he soon learned to write. Now he has to remember to write clumsily from time to time, or the master of the children would keep him at copying psalters without any chance for private reading. He dislikes Sundays and other feasts, when they must go outside the abbey and waste time in childish amusements. He is planning to read every book in the library.

But the library at St. Albans, though it is one of the better monastic libraries, does not contain a copy of every extant book written in Latin. Henry plans to read, one day, every Latin book in the world, which was quite a feasible program in the eleventh century. To do that he will have to travel. He is doing his best to map out his future.

When the time comes for his profession, he will refuse to take monastic vows. That will anger a great many people, but if he stands firm there is nothing they can do about it. His father will be furious; he vowed to dedicate his son to God because it seemed to him that God had showed him particular favor; now he will have to re-pay God in some other way. The cellarer of the abbey, though probably not the abbot, who never worries about money, will point out that for more than ten years St. Albans has lodged and fed Henry without payment, and taught him without charging a fee. He will have to promise to make some kind of repayment some day.

But when he refuses to become a monk he will have modern theological opinion on his side. Child oblates are now considered to be the wrong kind of recruit; a man should have a chance to see the secular world before he decides to leave it and embrace the religious life. Yet child oblates there must be, and in some quantity, for all monks should be literate and so far there is no machinery for teaching grown laymen who wish to enter the cloister how to read and write.

Henry will have to persuade a bishop to ordain him deacon. Someone would have to persuade a bishop anyway, since the abbot has no power of ordination; but whenever the Bishop of Lincoln calls at St. Albans he will ordain anyone recommended by the abbot. All the same, there is such a grave shortage of educated clerks that a bishop somewhere will take him into his family. There is the further point that he will not be reckoned dead to the world, as monks are reckoned. One day he may inherit a part of his father's property.

For the clerks in a bishop's family there is always plenty of work, all the increasing number of legal documents to be drawn up and copied. The new Norman kingdom of England is part of an international world, centered in Rome. Barons often choose wives from foreign countries. If any blood relationship can be traced between the parties, and baronial families preserve their pedigrees, there will have to be a dispensation from Rome. King William insists that his permission must be sought before any case is taken to Rome, but for a private matter that permission is seldom refused. If permission was not sought before the marriage there may be a question of an annulment, and that will end in Rome though it may begin in the diocesan court. Every man of substance leaves a written will; otherwise all his property would go to his natural heirs and no Masses would be offered for his soul. The bishop of the diocese is the natural custodian of all wills, and admits them to probate. During the last twenty years there has been a tremendous increase in the paperwork of every diocese, and an even greater increase in the written communications with Rome. Every bishop is clamoring for educated clerks. Once he is inside a bishop's family Henry will not seek for a country benefice. A rural parish is a dead end, fit only for some rustic English clerk who can barely stumble through the Missal. It is much smarter for a busy deacon to remain a deacon until he is consecrated bishop, and it is not unreasonable for Henry to hope for such promotion. During the twelfth century Gerald Barry, who very nearly became Archbishop of Menevia, remained a deacon until he died; and Thomas Becket, Chancellor of England, was ordained priest the day before he was consecrated Archbishop of Canterbury.

Some Norman laymen can read, but very few of them have acquired the laborious technique of writing. At the same time, more and more administrative and legal business is put down on paper. Every man of importance needs a clerk of his own.

Once he is free of St. Albans, Henry can be sure of a post. As a deacon he must remain celibate, though if he chooses to take a rustic parish no one will mind very much if he marries. Recently Rome has forbidden marriage to all priests of the Latin rite, but in the English countryside public opinion has nothing against married clergy, except that they must not try to make their benefices hereditary. A deacon suffers no legal disabilities except celibacy; in strict canon law he ought not to hunt or bear arms, but the life of Thomas Becket as Chancellor shows that these rules were not enforced. St. Thomas hawked and jousted, and no one took offense at it.

Henry may spend the rest of his life writing documents at the dictation of a bishop; but if he shows an aptitude for business he will soon become an archdeacon, collecting debts due to the diocese and judging cases of disputed wills and marriages. It is an important and well-rewarded post, involving constant travel with a large retinue of horses and servants, as we know from surviving complaints by those who were compelled to entertain archdeacons. If he is not quite good enough for a bishopric, with no important family influence behind him, there is always the King's service.

He remembers the visit of the Domesday commissioners a year ago. They were all clerks, able to read and write, even though they wrote a very ugly kind of shorthand of their own invention. They all drew good wages from the King. At Winchester there are a great many more clerks, constantly checking accounts for the King, as well as other clerks who travel every day with the traveling royal court. Some of these last are priests, who offer Mass daily in the royal chapel-tent; but essentially they are scribes. Then there are the King's servants, laymen and knights, who work for him as sheriffs and coroners; at least once a year they have to render account in writing. There is more writing in England than there has ever been before.

The advantage of an administration directed by bishops and staffed by deacons is that most of the cost is paid by the Church. If you consider the Church as a centralized institution, it draws a great revenue, a tithe of the gross product of the whole country; though out of this fund must come all the education in the country, all the char-

itable relief, all the repairs to roads and bridges (not an expensive item), *and* the support of all clerks. But the Church is not a centralized institution; the tithe from every field is allotted to some particular rector. Most of the clerks in the King's service are paid from the tithe of some benefice. As rectors they hire curates in priest's orders to do the actual parish work at a very small wage, while they themselves, as deacons, write letters for the King. That suits the King, who is always short of money. It angers the Pope, who frequently protests against the system, but he can do nothing worse than protest.

Ethelwulf, the third of our scholars, has decided after some heart-searching to continue with the monastic life. Perhaps his vocation is not very fervent, but he can see no place waiting for him in the secular world. He is descended from the ancient kings of Wessex, but only through younger sons. His grandfather was a king's thane, nearly as grand as an earl, but his father was a younger son and he himself has two elder brothers. If Ethelwulf does not become a monk he will probably dwindle into a free peasant. He will never be rich enough to equip himself with the horse and arms of a knight, no one wants a foot soldier, and a man of his blood cannot earn his bread by working with his hands.

He is not musical. He cannot get excited about the difference between the traditional English chant and the innovations from Normandy. He has heard, of course, that this subject led to actual fighting all over the choir and high altar at Glastonbury. What makes it worse is that the English lost, though the Norman abbot who

provoked them has been dismissed. The choirmonks de-
plore the bloodshed, though they hold that if ever civil
war should come to an abbey, which God forbid, a difference of opinion about the singing of the chant would
be a worthy cause to fight for.

Ethelwulf has never spoken with a choirmonk; when
choirmonks are permitted to talk, during worktime, they
talk only with one another. But the abbey is full of gos-
siping servants, glad to speak to someone of his noble
descent, and on Sunday rambles he often meets burgesses
from the town outside the gate. He knows that the community of St. Albans is divided between French and English, with the English by now a disappearing minority.
Abbot Paul is not so bad as some Normans. At least, in
the other great Anglo-French controversy, concerning the
monastic calendar of saints' days, he has thrown no
doubt upon the sanctity of their patron. But then Saint
Alban was a Roman, martyred by Roman pagans. They
say that at Canterbury, Archbishop Lanfranc sneered
at the holiness of Saint Alphege just because he was
English, although everyone remembers how he was martyred by heathen Danes only two generations ago. Some
of these foreigners cannot believe in their hearts that
any native Englishman can be worthy of Heaven.

As a monk of St. Albans, Ethelwulf will be more important than ever he would be in the secular world. As
things seem to be going, there is every chance that he
will not pass all his time in choir. In the good old days
of King Edward, the abbey lived on its rents. Peasants
paid it either in grain or in silver, and what they did with

the rest of their lives was a matter for the earl or his deputies. Under this new king, the landlord is responsible for order on his lands. In every manor there ought to be a court from time to time, and the lord or his steward ought to preside in it.

It is almost impossible to find lay stewards who are both competent and reasonably honest. The abbey would soon be insolvent if the prior did not send out some particular monk to manage the manor courts. Ever since the days of Saint Benedict, the traditional business manager of the community's property has been the cellarer, because the most expensive thing that every church has to buy is sacramental wine. Now the cellarer is excused attendance in choir because he has to spend so much of his time presiding in manor courts.

Sometimes there may be two courts on the same day, or there is some tricky agricultural innovation to be supervised. Then Abbot Paul will give some other monk an "obedience," commanding him to attend to the matter. The monk must be excused attendance in choir until his business is finished. There are more and more of these "obedientiary" monks, and their attendance in choir is becoming rare. Ethelwulf is interested in farming and law, two subjects worthy of the attention of any gentleman. He thinks he would be happy managing an estate.

Of the ruling officers of an abbey, the abbot is normally chosen from outside, by the King or the bishop or the archbishop; at any rate, by "the government." Of course, the monks have to go through the form of electing him in Chapter, according to the Rule of Saint Benedict, after he has been nominated by someone more powerful than they. But the prior, the second in command, and the cellarer, the business manager, are chosen by the abbot and community in Chapter. Ethelwulf reluctantly admits that henceforth all the abbots of St. Albans will probably be foreigners.

Probably the foreign abbot, if he has a strong personality, will nominate his prior. But he will hardly bother about the cellarer. The Chapter will choose him without outside pressure, and if they are wise they will choose an Englishman who can talk to their peasants. Most of the choirmonks will be foreigners who do not recognize the countless gradations of English society; but some will still be English, and even the foreigners will recall that Ethelwulf is nobly born according to English ideas. There is a very good chance that by the time Ethelwulf dies of old age he will have been for many years cellarer of St. Albans.

Even before that, he may be an obedientiary in charge of a manor, which would be very like ruling it as a secular lord. The present system of excusing a monk from choir for a day or two is unlikely to last. It means that the monk spends most of his time traveling. Very soon there will be more permanent obedientiaries, going out to some distant manor for a summer or for a whole year, perhaps hearing Mass in the local church on Sundays and living like laymen for the rest of the week. Yet they will still be monks, dedicated to religion and unspotted by the world. Ethelwulf wants to remain a regular, unlikely to be damned and with the prayers of the whole community to help him out of Purgatory if by bad luck he lands there. If all goes well he will have a good life, doing what he likes to do and yet doing it for the benefit of others. For the more revenue he gets out of the manor, the better will Saint Alban be served, with more candles on his altar, more splendid vestments, a more flourishing house.

Out of these three imaginary children of the cloister, one will be a good monk, one a good scholar, one a good businessman. Not one of them will do anything that would be wrong if a layman did it. Bad men do not often aspire to the religious life. The great danger in every abbey is not wickedness but slackness, making exceptions for today and then repeating them tomorrow.

Soon the monastic monopoly of education will vanish. Once the cathedral schools have begun to flourish and Oxford is a seat of learning, abbeys will become more and more business concerns. Choirmonks will be a humble rank and file, ruled by busy obedientiaries. To get up in the middle of the night to chant the full Office will be merely a tiresome preliminary to the serious business of monastic life, the management of a flourishing estate. But by that time all novices will be grown men.

V · THE PEASANTS

The trouble with Normans, as the whole village grumbles, is that they cannot tell one Englishman from another. Last year there was this visit from the Domesday commissioners, and on the whole it did more good than harm. The custom of the manor has been written down, and the record has been lodged with the King, who has no direct interest in how much the lord makes from his tenants and will very likely do justice if you can get him to listen to you.

Of course, the commissioners did not stay here very long. The ground had been well prepared before they arrived, and they saw only what they expected to see. First of all, the lord's steward went to the shire court. There he explained to the sheriff the exact boundaries of all his lord's holdings within the shire, what he got from the land, and what he ought to pay the King for it, in *geld* and military service. That was a matter between the lord and the King of England, both Normans, and it hardly affected the English villagers.

Then the parish priest and four honest men of the village went to the hundred court, where the sheriff was still inquiring into the working of the manor. They told the sheriff how much each of the villagers ought to pay the lord, and the sheriff checked it with what the lord's steward had told him earlier. The two estimates agreed fairly well, and the parish priest smoothed over any discrepancies to the general satisfaction. All the same, this deputation brought back unwelcome news. The system of frankpledge is going to be enforced most strictly, by the lord's steward in the manor court. This is a very ancient system for keeping the peace, or rather for getting money out of those who have broken it. All male adult peasants are supposed to be divided into groups of ten men, called tithings, and if one of them should be fined for breaking the law, the other nine will be responsible for seeing that the fine is paid. Frankpledge is very ancient. The tradition goes that it existed in this part of Wessex, the shire of Southampton, before King Alfred began to fight the Danes. But in the good old days of King Edward no one bothered to enforce it, and, of course, during the nine months when King Harold held the throne there was no peace to be kept. Now the fines for being out of frankpledge will be paid to the Norman lord, who notoriously exacts every penny of his rights. Every peasant must join one of these tithings or pay a fine at each meeting of the manor court. Each tithing must appoint a tithingman to be responsible for all of them—an invidious job, which no one is eager to undertake.

This reinforcement of frankpledge seems at first sight to be a sensible regulation. It is broadly in line with the promise King William made at his coronation. At that time he swore to maintain the good laws of King Edward, and so he does; but these laws are now enforced to the letter, whereas King Edward often let them slide. So far the Norman king has changed nothing except a good many titles to land. The purely military regulation that landholders must come to the muster mounted and in complete mail is a regulation which affects Normans only, and those few English landholders who have thrown in their lot with the Normans.

No, these Normans acted righteously, in their own estimation. They never spotted the reason why frankpledge was dropping out of use. That is, of course, because in an average manor it is impossible to find ten adult males of the same social standing. Englishmen divide themselves naturally into classes, and do not care to be made responsible for the behavior of their social inferiors.

No one was able to explain this to the commissioners during their brief visit to the manor. They investigated the land, and who held how much of it, and from that they drew a few broad distinctions. It was not their fault that they went back in time no farther than the reign of King Edward; in that they were only following their instructions. But how much land a man holds now, and what return he gives to the lord for permission to hold it, are not the most important elements in the status of a villager. What matters much more, in the eyes of his neighbors, is how he came to hold it.

This is a large and prosperous manor in northern Hampshire, big enough to make up a whole parish. The lord is a powerful baron, holding estates all over England; he seldom comes near his Hampshire manor, and his steward normally presides in the manor court. But there is a hall, big enough for the lord if ever he chooses to come, and a granary to hold the stored grain from the demesne. The steward lives in the hall with his family, though if the lord should arrive he would move out with his wife and children, to camp in a corner of the granary until the visit ended. There are also two neighboring socmen, considerable landholders. They pay a small rent in money for their land, and take their disputes to the manor court. All this the commissioners could understand, and they got it down quite accurately.

But they divided all the other villagers into two classes. Men who held enough land to support a family in comfort were put down as *villani*, peasants; men who held a bit of land, but who had to work for wages to make ends meet, were *cottarii*, smallholders. The plowman who works whole time on the demesne, and holds no land for himself, was enrolled as a slave; which is more or less accurate, though as a Christian parishioner he has certain personal rights. For example, if he marries without the permission of his lord the marriage will stand, for marriage is a sacrament and no Christian may be denied access to the sacraments; and his owner may not kill him without just cause, for in law that is reckoned murder.

So the slave is not really a slave in the old Roman sense, though he is enrolled as a *servus*, the Latin word for slave. He may not, of course, be sold by his lord, against his will.

But the *villani*, the villagers, the peasants, come from many different backgrounds. What the commissioners noted was that each family held about thirty acres of land, and that instead of paying a rent reckoned in money they worked for the lord with their own hands, on a certain number of days in the week.

That is broadly true, and it seems a simple statement. But the simple statement conceals a number of traps. In the first place, an acre need not be the same size as any other acre. It is not a measure of area, but rather a measure of work done; it is the amount of land that can be plowed by an eight-ox team in one day. That varies, of course, according to the stiffness of the soil, and the number of tree stumps and boulders in it; or perhaps according to the difficulties of plowing it in the days when the West Saxons first came to these parts some centuries ago. For an acre remains an acre as the ancestors of these villagers first reckoned it. Just to make things more tricky, hardly anyone uses an eight-ox team nowadays, unless the soil is very stiff indeed. Continued tillage, and perhaps an improvement in the design of plows, have made a six-ox team sufficient for most purposes. Hardly any individual peasant owns as many as six oxen; most of them have two oxen, a yoke, and must make up their teams by co-operating with their neighbors.

The amount of work on the demesne demanded for a full holding also varies without any apparent reason. It is the labor of a single man and usually of a yoke of oxen; by now it has crystallized into the custom of the manor. One explanation of the variation in the amount of labor demanded from similar holdings is that long ago a peasant with several grown-up sons could give more than a child-less bachelor. But in fact, we can only guess at the reason. Certainly it has nothing to do with the comparative fer-tility of the land.

Then, how many hours of work are there in a day's labor? In general a peasant works so long as it is light enough to work, eight hours in midwinter, sixteen hours in midsummer. But it has been suggested that the average day of weekwork on the lord's demesne should end at noon, and that the peasant may cultivate his own holding after dinner. Once again, the commissioners just don't know.

Suppose that on the days when work is due to be done on the demesne the steward has nothing in particular that needs doing? Again, custom varies from village to village. In some places the peasants are lucky and can take the day off; in others they have to pay work-silver, a day's wages, to make up what they owe. It is fairly cer-tain that in most places at most times the peasant can offer work-silver instead of coming himself, if he happens to have the money to spare. But the lord's steward has the right to demand work instead of money; he may demand it because there are no idle hands to hire, or indeed just to stop the peasant getting above himself. In the eleventh century a right that is not exercised will soon be considered obsolete.

There are three periods in the year when every hand is needed in the fields: the plowing in the winter, the sowing in the spring, and the harvest in August and September. For plowing, all the strong men and all the oxen must turn out, to work all day until all the land in the village has been opened. It is the same for spring sowing, and often for the harrowing to rid the field of weeds. The harvest, the greatest event of the year, needs not only all the men but all the mobile women and children also. At these busy seasons the villagers do boonwork, which is more strenuous and lasts for longer hours than the ordinary weekwork. The Latin for these boondays is *beneficia*, from which we may get our modern word "beanfeast." If the whole village is reaping the harvest, wives as well as men, the steward will provide a communal dinner for them.

We know of these boondays only from records of what work was due to be done on the lord's demesne. But it is very likely that the peasants continued at the same strenuous tempo until the main village field in use that year had been completely covered. If no peasant owned a complete plow-team, he must have worked with his neighbors, and he would want to see his neighbor's land plowed and sown nearly as badly as he wanted to finish his own. If there was not enough to eat in the village, he would have to share the loss with his neighbor.

In the village we are discussing there are two common fields, though some places have three. Every year one is left fallow, and the other is plowed and sown. There are no fences to divide the separate holdings. Instead, narrow strips called balks are left unplowed between them. Each acre is the length of a furlong, as long as oxen can conveniently plow without turning. Nowadays that has been standardized at 220 yards, but in the eleventh century it varied with the stiffness of the soil. The holding of each peasant would probably be scattered in strips about the field, so that everyone got his share of fertile and bad soil. You can see that if a peasant allowed his land to go unweeded or unplowed, his neighbors would suffer also, which was one incentive to neighborly help.

But though everyone works together, that does not mean that all workers are equal, any more than in a modern office all the clerks sitting side by side in a large room are equal. Perhaps the lord and his steward see them as roughly equal, each holding about the same amount of land and giving roughly the same amount of work for it; but in the village itself everyone knows that some peasants are on the way up and others on the way down.

About noon on a weekday in July 1087, a group of men are sitting in the shade of a tree, eating their dinner of bread and cheese. They have been working all morning in the common field, clearing weeds from the edges of the strips and making sure that the balks between the strips are free of obstacles; in a few days the reaping will begin, and there must be nothing to hinder the movements of the reapers. It is one of the days when no one is compelled to work on the lord's demesne, so they have all been working on their own land. They all have more or less the same dinner, though the quality of the bread may differ. They are all dressed in much the same way: stout leg bandages to protect their calves from thorns, bare feet, low-necked woolen shirts which come nearly to the knee. Under the shirts they wear woolen drawers, for decency's sake, but these are not apparent. Each has a rope girdle at his waist, from which hangs the wallet that recently carried his dinner. Some wear wide-brimmed straw hats, either on their heads or dangling from a string at the back of their necks. When they came to work in the chill of dawn, they were wrapped in thick frieze cloaks with hoods attached, but they have taken these off and left them in the sun to air as the day grew warmer. They have never shaved in their lives, and nature has taken its course with their hair, beards, and mustaches. Each of them gives off a powerful stink of sweat, dirt, and unwashed wool; but that is characteristic of everyone who works on the land, and their neighbors do not notice it.

They recline under the shade of the same tree as they take their siesta. By their sides are their jealously guarded tools, iron sickles and spades and wooden rakes, of very much the same design as those used by hedge cutters in the twentieth century. But they are not, after all, sitting in one group.

Ulf the slave is not there at all. He works all day on the lord's demesne, and at dinnertime he goes to the hall kitchen, where he usually gets a hot dinner, better food than the free peasants have eaten. But he has to eat it in the byre beside the oxen who are his chief care, because nobody cares to sit beside him in the hall. He has not been able to find a girl in the village willing to marry him, though if he found one the priest would be willing to marry them. While he is fit to work he probably lives better than some free peasants. But when he is old and doddering, his lord will probably free him, and then, without land of his own, he will be in danger of death from starvation. While he drives his oxen he looks like a scarecrow, half-naked and with his few clothes full of holes; he has no woman to mend them for him, no family of any kind.

Three cottars are sitting together, sharing their bread and cheese. They have been working for a wage on the land of another, for their own little holdings will not feed them all the year round. At this time of year it is hard to get a job, and they have been lucky. July, when everyone is getting to the bottom of last year's stores, is always a hard time for the villagers. But very soon it will be time to reap the harvest; if the crops are good everyone will want extra hands, and there will be wages and food and plenty of ale for all comers.

But though these three cottars sit together, even they do not regard themselves as exactly equal. They cannot forget that Egbert had a grandfather who was a socman, and that he came down in the world through no fault of his own. The socman was very heavily fined in the shire court; some say he had been caught robbing on the highway, but the version Egbert prefers is that single-handed he killed three men in fair fight and then had to pay three *weres*. Anyway, he sold most of his land. Egbert's father had only a little plot for himself, just a garden of cabbages and two strips in the open field. Egbert takes any job he can get and saves his wages. He hopes to be able to buy more land one day. He takes great care never to seem proud of his noble ancestry, but his companions cannot forget it.

Burhed, the second cottar, had a grandfather who was a slave. Of course, he was free by the time he came to die; most of the slaves in England are freed when they are past work. That is not charity, or a reward for faithful service; it is because no sensible lord wants to support an old man who cannot earn his keep. But the lord of Burhed's grandfather made an error of judgment. The slave had been savaged by a bull, and his leg so badly broken that it was the general opinion that he would never walk again. He had to be carried on a litter to the parish church so that the priest might formally pronounce him free and responsible for earning his own living. Whereupon the cripple made an astonishing recovery, married a young girl who liked him, and hobbled off to the edge of the waste to clear a little patch of ground. Burhed's grandfather was very lame for the rest of his life, but he lived to a great age and left a small square field to his descendants. Such a new field is called an assart, and usually it is free of labor dues. But a few years ago the tidy-minded steward of the new Norman lord persuaded Burhed's father to throw it into one of the common fields and accept in exchange a few strips of plowland. Burhed is on the way up, as Egbert is on the way down. But what the village remembers is the condition of their ancestors, and Burhed will never be esteemed the true equal of the grandson of a socman.

Nobody knows the ancestry of Thorfinn, the third of the cottars. His father turned up on the manor thirty years ago, in the days of good King Edward. He was meanly dressed and he had no money at all, but he carried a battle-ax over one shoulder. He said, of course, that he had found it in the forest and thought it too valuable to leave lying in the path. But he carried it as though he had carried such things before. The English lord who ruled then, until he picked the wrong side to fight for at Hastings, wanted more able-bodied men about the place. He bought the ax from the stranger, and allowed him a cottage and a few strips of land in exchange. After he had been in the manor some years on probation, the stranger was accepted by his neighbors, but he never talked about his past. Presently he married a local girl, but of all his children only this one son grew up. The priest when Thorfinn was born had a fad against English names. He said that everyone ought to be baptized with a name that had already been borne by a saint. So the boy was baptized John, but his father and mother never called him anything but Thorfinn: a heathenish name, but then everyone had already guessed that his father had been a Viking, shipwrecked and on the run. Now the village has got used to the queer name, and only strangers notice it. But then, how many strangers ever learn the name of a cottar who does not travel? The Domesday commissioner who wrote it down in his big book made a grimace when he first heard it. But then he was a Norman, and probably there was a Thorfinn among his own Viking ancestors a couple of centuries ago, so he let it pass.

Thorfinn is a quiet, peaceable man, though very strong and nimble. The villagers still think of him as half a foreigner, because his father came from the great outside world whence come all the enemies who ravage peaceful manors. But so long as he never puts forward an opinion of his own, they are resigned and accustomed to his presence.

These three cottars, of such unequal ancestry and background, ought to be in the same tithing of frank-pledge. Naturally, they dislike the prospect, and they have already made a private agreement that if one of them should break the law the others will not be expected to contribute to the sum to be paid. But if these foolish Normans, who can't even speak English properly, want to see all the peasants lined up in groups of ten, then they are quite willing to swear they are in the same tithing, for the sake of peace and quiet.

In the shade of the same tree, though forming a separate group, a score of full villagers are dozing. They are respectable, independent men who normally never do anything so low as to work for wages. Each holds enough land to feed his family throughout the year and to occupy him every day, with the necessary weekwork and boon-work for the lord. Of course, they also come from differ-ent backgrounds, and each independent peasant really forms a social class with only one member. But the lord's steward persists in regarding them as a group, and be-cause they so often have to act as a group they have acquired a certain group sentiment.

All are suitors of equal worth in the manor court. The manor court, which meets once a month, wastes a lot of time in fining people for petty offenses, deeds which the suitors do not think really blameworthy, though for fear of the lord's steward they have to inflict a punishment. There are other formal ceremonies, such as transferring the land of a dead man to his rightful heir, acknowledg-ing the rights of widows, or ratifying tenancies already concluded between some newcomer and the lord's stew-ard. But the suitors of the manor court also take mean-ingful and important decisions. They fix the dates for the plowing, the sowing, the harvesting. In the open fields of the village such things must be done by all hus-bandmen at the same time.

Once a year the suitors of the manor court have the distasteful task of selecting one of their number as reeve. Nobody wants that job, though on its face it looks pleas-ant. The reeve is rather like a foreman. It is his duty to see that every man really works on the demesne when he ought to be working, that he is not merely physically present, leaning gracefully on a spade. The reeve himself is excused labor, because all his time should be taken up with overseeing. His badge of office is a long cane, with which he stimulates idlers. Presumably he officiated in the same way at the communal sowing, reaping, and plowing, though the records are only concerned with what happened on the lord's demesne. In fact, besides being a foreman he is a kind of unofficial works police-man. It sounds a pleasant way of life for a lazy man, making others work while he does no work himself. The catch is that it lasts for only one year. The ex-reeve will have to live for the rest of his life with the peasants he has been driving, and the new reeve will take particular trouble to see that he does his full share of the work.

The job is so unpopular that no one is willing to serve. In later times no free peasant would take it, and evidence that a man had been a reeve was taken as conclusive proof that he was a serf. This uncertainty about status is chiefly the fault of the Domesday commissioners. They had to invent a technical terminology as they went along, for an inquiry of this kind had never been held before. Every peasant they found with a full share in the village field, who owed suit to the manor court and paid for his land by personal service, they wrote down as a *villanus*. Some of these men had been free, merely giving personal service instead of a money rent because they found it more convenient. But by about A.D. 1200 *villanus* had been rendered into French as *villein*, and the Latin for that was *servus*. An appeal to the evidence of Domesday Book would prove that all the men of the manor were serfs, even if some of them protested that their ancestors had been free. But *servus* could only mean serf, because by that date there were no genuine slaves in England. It is an improvement that we owe to the Norman Conquest. During the reign of good King Edward there were more slaves in England than in any other country of Western Christendom.

Among the peasants who have been lying in the shade is Godric, son of Godric. For several generations that name has been given to the eldest sons of his family. It is by far the commonest name used by Englishmen, so that Normans who want to make fun of a Norman too keen to adopt English ways use it as a nickname. Godric has a full holding in the village fields. He is a respected member of the community, chiefly because his family have been in these parts for time out of mind. He is thirty-five years of age, but his mother died some time ago and his father last year, so that he is now head of his household. Peasants normally marry young, for as soon as they are old enough to work with the men they are as well off as they will ever be. Godric has a son aged sixteen, of course known to all the village as Young Godric; his fourteen-year-old daughter is called Godgifu after her mother, and his youngest surviving child is a twelve-year-old boy named Godmund. Godgifu is as common a name for English women as Godric is for men, and the younger boy's name has the same first syllable so that everyone will know the family he comes from.

When the sun is lower and the day not quite so hot, Godric and his two sons continue their work in the barley field. All the peasants feel a suppressed excitement. The harvest is nearly ready, and it promises to be good. It looks as if there will be enough grain to feed the whole village until next year and to be brewed into abundant ale. The villagers have done all that they should, but no one can guarantee a good harvest until it has been reaped. They know they are in the hands of God. In all villages the proportion of regular churchgoers is higher than in towns.

The manor court will meet next week, and among other things will fix the time for reaping to begin. It must come soon, and it will be the greatest event of the year. A bad harvest means hunger for all; most elderly men have lived through it more than once. Nothing but water to drink, since grain is too precious for brewing; water-drinking usually brings an epidemic of disease, though the men who empty their rubbish into the nearest stream cannot imagine why. During the cold of January, babies and the very old die; for when there is not enough food for all, the fit young men must be kept strong for the spring plowing. Perhaps the lord or the parish priest will distribute some bread in charity; but their income also comes from the land, and in a bad season they will have little to spare. If a manor near by has an abundance, some wagon-loads of corn will be imported; but it is not likely that a nearby manor will have anything to spare, since it will have shared the same weather. With the roads so narrow and twisted it would be impossible to bring in corn from afar, apart from the great expense; besides, if the famine were widespread, someone would steal the corn on the way.

Everyone has heard that there are magical means of making the crops fail, though no one round here would

be so wicked as to practice them. If there were a magical way to ensure a good harvest, that would be more of a temptation. Luckily for the spiritual welfare of the peasants, there is none, though some narrow-minded parish priests sometimes denounce corn dollies and midsummer bonfires.

But this is going to be a good harvest, unless within the next ten days a storm strikes. Everything must be in perfect order for the great day. Godric walks through all the balks between the plots in the field, cutting tall grasses with his bagging hook, grubbing up weeds with his mattock, knocking down nettles with anything handy. Sharp stones must be removed, lest they wound the bare feet of the reapers. Already a comrade has pointed out a sunny south-sloping corner of the field where the wheat seems ripe enough to be reaped for Lammas, the Loaf-Mass. The Lammas loaf is baked from the first wheat of the new harvest, and consecrated by the parish priest in the first Mass offered after it has been made. It is an earnest that there really will be a harvest this year, as there was last year. It cannot be a feast of the Universal Church, for the date of this early prophet of the harvest varies from district to district throughout Christendom. But to the villagers it is nearly as great a feast as Easter.

Young Godric has spent the afternoon turning a grindstone to sharpen the sickles. He is strong enough to keep at it, and it is work traditionally suited to a young boy who will presently hold land in the field. He has set up his machine just by a corner of the field, so that the barley may recognize what will soon happen to it. Every villager with a full share in the field has come up to have his sickle sharpened on this lucky spot, even if it is sharp enough already. The barley is not eager to die, of course, but it ought to know that it was sown by the villagers to feed the whole village; and if the barley knows that it is fulfilling its appointed destiny, the harvesting will go off without accident. There are no heathen customs in this good Christian village, but that is no reason to flout ancient habits that bring good luck. A few years ago they did without the sickle-sharpening, because a visiting priest said it was nothing less than devil-worship. Then one of the reapers stumbled and stuck his sickle into his leg. He bled to death before anyone could stanch the wound, which proved that the visiting priest had been talking nonsense.

Godmund has been scaring birds from the ripe grain. Just before harvest they become very impudent. He is supposed to do it with a wooden clapper, and by shouting at the robbers. But in fact, the rope girdle wound twice round his shirt can be used as a sling, and when he knows that the lord's steward is busy somewhere else out of sight he sometimes slings a stone at a pigeon. That is quite against the law. The only pigeons near by belong to the lord, who has a pigeoncote beside his hall. The lord's pigeons are entitled to feed on the grain growing in the village field, and no one else is allowed to keep domestic pigeons. If the steward saw what Godmund was at, his father could be made to pay a heavy fine, but no villager who saw him would tell tales. During the afternoon Godmund manages to knock over two pigeons, and hides their bodies under a convenient thornbush. He dare not poach more than two, for fear the steward might notice that some were missing.

Tonight those pigeons will go into the family cooking pot, if Godmund plucks them first and takes the trouble to bury the feathers. He is feeling very hungry. Even though they had a good harvest last year, bread is running short during these last few days before the next harvest. What is left must go to his father and his elder brother, to keep up their strength for the work they must do. His own dinner is only a very small oatcake and a wad of greenstuff.

An hour before sunset all the villagers go home from the field. During the afternoon there was little for them to do, but they could not bear to leave the crop which will be their mainstay for the next year. They have tended the paths and prepared their tools, and now they are aching to begin harvesting.

Godric's house is a one-roomed cabin, without furniture. But in fact it satisfies all his needs. It is used only for sleeping, and on part of the floor is a pile of straw bedding covered with old clothes where the whole family sleep every night in a row. Its walls are of timber and clay, and its thatched roof extends all round in wide eaves. In the middle of the single room is a flat hearthstone, with above it a hole in the thatch to let out some of the smoke. The rest of the smoke stays permanently inside and blackens the inside walls. There are no windows, and the doorless entry can be closed with a leather curtain. That makes it very warm, smelly, and smoky on winter nights, when all the family huddle together in the wide bed. At this time of year, on a dry and windless July night, they will all sleep outside under the eaves.

In summer the wide eaves make it really into a three-room cottage. At the back is another hearthstone, where Godgifu does the cooking in calm weather. The porch under the eaves in front makes a parlor, where the family may gossip with their neighbors. At the sides and back is a little garden plot, where they grow cabbage and lettuce and where the domestic washing may be spread out to dry. At the far end of this garden are a pigsty and some henhouses, for Godric is one of the more prosperous villagers. If this cabin and garden were on a desert island it would supply all their ordinary needs, except for bread-grain and blacksmith's work.

Godgifu and her daughter are waiting for the men. They have just kindled a fire with furze and peat by the back porch, and the big black iron pot is filled with water. The iron pot is their most valuable possession, the only one of their household goods that would be worth mentioning in an inventory. The pot, an iron fork, and a long iron spoon are Godgifu's only cooking utensils, except for a few expendable wooden spoons, thrown away when they are too badly charred or split. Because the men took only a cold snack to the fields they will have their hot meal in the evening. No villager ever eats more than one cooked meal a day. Since the new laws were proclaimed to protect the King's forest, firewood is very hard to come by.

In this warm July weather Godgifu and her daughter

wear no more than long shifts with kirtles over them, though each keeps in the house a big frieze cloak with a hood attached, for cold weather. They are accustomed to going barefoot all the year round, though when the ground is covered with snow or deep in mud they may put on high pattens, or clogs, to keep their toes out of the wet. But their heads and necks are always covered up, with dark woolen kerchiefs tied under the chin. All their clothes are of wool, and might in theory be washed. But it is simpler to keep one kirtle for best and wash it fairly often. A peasant girl would be putting on airs above her station if the clothes which she wore working in the fields were not grubby.

Today, with harvest so near, all the women of the village have been cleaning out the threshing floor. That is a place used only once a year, and it gets very muddy and dirty in winter, but the village could not exist without it.

Threshing, like everything else connected with harvest, is one of the highlights of the year. It is very hard work. All the strong men of the village bang away at the harvested crop with long flails, made of two pieces of wood joined by a hinge of leather thong and weighted with lumps of rock. Against the stone of the threshing floor their blows separate the grain from the straw. Unless there happens to be a strong breeze blowing, the girls stand by with winnowing fans, which will blow the chaff away from the much heavier grain. Even if there is a good breeze the girls will be standing round. This is one of the occasions when the men of the village will be working side by side, and the strongest among them may display their muscle to impress their future brides.

A flail, by the way, is the nearest thing to a deadly weapon that most villagers possess. Certainly a man knocked down by a flail is unlikely to get up again. But it is more useful for a lynching than for battle. Any swordsman or pikeman can kill a peasant before the peasant can lift his flail. The villagers think of themselves as unarmed and useless for war, and because they think so it is true, though long ago their ancestors drove the Welsh from Hampshire.

Lammas will begin the gayest and most interesting period of the year, which continues right up to Christmas. First there will be the harvesting with all its attendant jollifications, the carrying in of the corn dolly and the great supper of harvest home. Michaelmas, the twenty-ninth of September, is the end of the agricultural year. The lord's steward will make up his accounts on that day, and reckon with all the villagers to make sure they have rendered their services. Some villagers will have to pay silver in lieu; others will be forgiven. There is really no rule in this matter. It all depends on how prosperous the steward is feeling at the time.

Then will begin the great slaughter of the beasts. From harvest to Michaelmas the stubble on the village field is thrown open for grazing. There is more grazing than we might expect nowadays, for men reaping by hand with short sickles cut off little more than the ears and leave the straw long; of course the other field, left fallow this year, has been grazed since the grass began to grow in the spring. But only a narrow strip of water meadow is mown for hay, which is always scarce and very precious. Roots are not planted as cattle food. Once the grass has stopped growing in the autumn, all superfluous animals must be killed.

Naturally, some must be left alive, to carry on the stock —a few young cows and at least one bull. On many manors there is only one bull; the parish priest, who does not go out to work in the field, keeps an eye on him. Then there are the working oxen, without which the fields could not be tilled. Godric owns a yoke of oxen, which means that as a peasant he is fairly prosperous. He shares with his neighbors to make up a team. The only complete team on the manor is owned by the lord, and looked after by his solitary slave.

Godric also owns his share of the village sheep and pigs, a share carefully limited by the size of his holding in the field. But he does not look after them in person. His sheep graze in the waste with the village flock; his pigs root in the woods with the other swine of the village, in the care of wholetime guardians. The village shepherd and the village swineherd are fairly important members of the community, rewarded for their work by extra holdings in the village fields. Who worked these holdings is obscure: perhaps the villagers as a whole, perhaps members of the family of the holder.

When Michaelmas comes round it will be for Godric to say which of his beasts are destined for slaughter, bearing in mind that in winter grazing will be very short. Most of the young animals will be killed, at a time when they are fat and in good condition after the plentiful autumn grazing.

All the men of the village will join in the killing. It is an exciting occasion, in rather a horrid way, and they will make a holiday of it. After the beasts have been killed and skinned, the carcasses will be cut into pieces and thoroughly rubbed with salt. Then the joints will be put up in wooden casks, with a great deal more salt added. It is to be hoped that the salt beef and salt pork will not become so putrid as to be quite uneatable until fresh meat becomes available again in the spring.

Naturally, a mere villager can seldom afford to eat his own meat. These casks are portable wealth, fairly easy to sell for money. They are sold to the lord, to other rich men, or in town markets. But generally speaking, the meat is paid for. A villager owes labor, and occasional odd pennies, to his lord, but he very seldom owes a rent reckoned in salt meat.

This has not always been so. In the early days of the English settlement, when kingdoms were small and numerous, the King and his court would move from village to village, eating the produce on the spot. This village is still burdened with what was in origin two days' supplies for the royal household; but by the eleventh century it is reckoned in money and the sheriff collects it from the lord. Of course, the lord has collected it in the first place from his tenants, either in silver or in kind.

Everything that the peasants pay, in money or in labor, goes first to the lord's steward. They have no idea what happens to it afterwards. They believe that the King has a lot of money tucked away somewhere, and that he ought to live off his own—so there will certainly be trouble when in future days their descendants encounter national taxation.

After the jollifications of Michaelmas, when there is usually plenty of meat about and by rights all debts should have been settled, work on the land is fairly light. The harvested field will lie fallow for a year; in the other field some land will be plowed for winter wheat. There will be the usual unending struggle against encroaching weeds. But the days are growing shorter and no one can work after dark; granaries seem full. It is a time for sitting by the fire and telling stories, and there is better to come. Christmas is the only holiday of the year and it lasts until Epiphany. During the Twelve Days of Christmas nobody does any work and everyone who can afford it eats as much as he can hold. Immediately after Christmas the spring plowing begins, everyone notices that there is not so much bread left to last until harvest as he had supposed, and steady work in the fields rises to a crescendo until another Lammas comes.

But this is a July evening in 1087, and getting on for suppertime. Already there is a harvest feeling in the air, and all the Godric family feel cheerful. Godgifu fills the iron pot with barley meal, greenstuff, and miscellaneous fruit and berries; Godmund slips in his two plucked pigeons, and young Godgifu proudly contributes half a rabbit that she and another girl found in a snare. This is the hungry season, when the granaries are almost bare and every villager eats anything he can get. But soon the fields will be reaped and there will be plenty for all.

Unfortunately, there is very little barley left for brewing into ale. Ale without hops will not keep for much longer than a fortnight at most, and perhaps that is a good thing; otherwise there might be a temptation to brew huge quantities of ale after harvest and go short of bread for some months of next summer. Godgifu fills wooden or horn mugs for all her household, but what she puts in is very pale and thin. Even so it is better than water from the stream, for when it was brewed it was brought to the boil. It is a curious but unexplained fact that people who drink water often die from sudden pains in the stomach.

The stew also is watery and thin, though they can just taste the pigeons. But though this is not a very satisfying meal, there is plenty to talk about, for the family have not been assembled together since they went off to their work soon after dawn.

Godric and his sons have been working in the same field, but it is a big field and since the noon halt they have not seen much of one another. The boys have not yet heard the full story of what the lord's steward said to Godric just before he finished work. It is very hard luck, and all the worse because the steward would not explain it properly, though he speaks very good English—for a Norman—since he has been in the village for at least fifteen years. There is a little argument on this last point. Years are hard to reckon, since each is so like the last, but in the end they all agree it was fifteen years if not more.

Early tomorrow morning Godric is to yoke up his pair of oxen to an empty cart and take them to the market town about eight miles off. Oxen travel at a little less than two miles an hour, so they will hardly arrive before midday. The steward will start much later, after seeing the work properly begun on the demesne; but since he rides a hackney which can cover six miles in an hour, he will overtake Godric as he arrives. In the town Godric will load his cart with something or other before bringing it back to the village. But the steward explained that he could not remember the English name for what was to be fetched.

That is most tiresome. Godric cannot grumble at being sent on the errand. His oxen owe labor to the lord just as he does, and in a way it is a compliment to be trusted with this responsibility. If the oxen have to work from dawn to dusk it will count as two weekworks, and he will gain a day. But it is maddening not to know what they must haul, and especially how long it will take to load the cart. It cannot be anything very heavy, or the steward would have sent more than two oxen. But how long will it take to load? Will it be lying in a heap all ready for him? Or will it be a lot of little things that have to be bought one at a time and then loaded carefully because they are fragile? Worst of all would be pots and dishes for the hall table, most of them imported from France, and that seems most likely. In that case Godric will pass the afternoon hanging about in the market, with no money of his own to spend at this hungriest season of the year; and if he starts for home late in the day he will have to sleep the night on the road. Oxen cannot be hurried.

Godgifu points out that Godric should start off prepared for the worst. He must take his frieze cloak to sleep in. She can give him enough bread and cheese for a day and a night, though after that there will be very little left at home. He must take the flint and steel, in case he can find fuel to make a fire by the roadside. There is only one steel in the house, but if the cooking fire should go out she can always borrow a burning brand from a neighbor. He must carry a good sharp knife, and instead of gaping at fripperies in the market he should keep a hold of his oxen; anything may be stolen in that wicked foreign town. Godric replies that he has not been called up for a campaign; the only advantage of being a villager is that no one ever tells you to fight. But he will remember her advice, and take care that those wicked burgesses do not steal his oxen.

All these troubles spring from the foreignness of the steward. Why can't he speak proper English, as do all honest men? But he manages the manor very cleverly, better than did his predecessor in the days of good King Edward; these Normans know all the latest dodges in agriculture. And after all, the old steward was really a foreigner; he was a Dane from the other side of Watling Street, full of the most ridiculous ideas that might suit his native fens but would never do in Hampshire. You could understand what he said, but he used Danish names for all the tools and the different kinds of seed, so that very often you understood wrong. Godric and his wife shake their heads, remembering some absurd mix-ups of their youth. That was long ago, before they were married. None of the children can remember England ruled by an English king. Nobody mentions the Norman lord, or wonders whether he can understand any English. He never visits this manor for more than a night or two in the year, and has made no impression on his villagers.

Godric has trouble in remembering the past. Every year is so like every other. He was born in this cabin, and he expects to die in it. It is not exactly the cabin of his childhood. The straw on the roof and the plaster of the walls do not last much more than ten years, and he has seen them renewed more than once. But the crucks at each end, the curved posts leaning together which hold up all the rest, they are his home. If he had to move to some other spot—but why should he ever move?—he would take these four crooked poles with him and it would still be his old home. They never wear out. His grandfather told him that they had been chosen for their convenient shape by one of the first English settlers in these parts.

He has never been away from home for more than a night or two, and he never expects to be. Once, with a flock of other children, he went to Winchester to be confirmed, guided by an energetic parish priest. That was the longest journey of his life, still remembered by all his contemporaries. None of his own children has been confirmed, because later rectors have lacked the initiative to organize such an expedition. There are very few bishops in England, and most of the villagers have never seen one in their lives. Perhaps one day some bishop may come within walking distance of the village, and then all the peasants will come out to meet him; but most of them will die without Confirmation, which is not essential to salvation.

Godric has seen his secular lord, but not very frequently. The lord spends most of his time at his castle in Sussex or at his other castle on the March of Wales, the frontier between Wales and England, though as a rule he passes through this manor once or twice a year during his incessant traveling. If Godric gets mixed up in a lawsuit too important to be settled by the manor court, he may have to journey to the Sussex castle, which is the head of the whole barony; but with any luck he will never have to go so far. He has never seen the King. Once the court rode by within a few miles, but it was the season of the spring plowing and he could not spare the time to go and cheer as all the lords rode by. He has never wanted to travel. He likes to keep an eye on his own oxen, his own pigs, his own strips in the field. He likes to meet strangers if they are men of his own kind, English peasants from Wessex. Men from beyond the Thames, whether English or Danish, speak a different kind of language and he regards them as foreigners. But men of his own kind seldom travel, so he seldom chats with a stranger. His is a very small world, but he is perfectly adjusted to it. He is a respected figure in the village, he supports himself and his family from his own land, he has never been in trouble with the law. He expects to live in his own cabin until he dies of old age; his first serious illness will carry him off, since there is no medical attention within reach. Then he will be buried, without headstone or coffin, in the consecrated patch of ground by the church where the bones of his ancestors already lie scattered in disorder.

When he is dead his eldest son Godric will inherit his share of the field. The lord's steward will take the better of his two oxen as a heriot, a kind of death duty. The lord is entitled to the best beast left by any of his dead peasants, and no one will object. Young Godric will have to buy another ox to make up the team, but all the villagers have to buy their oxen from time to time, since no one owns a herd of cattle for breeding. There are already a few silver pennies buried in a box under the floor of the cabin for that very purpose. Then young Godric will be presented to the manor court as the new tenant, and as soon as he has been recognized a new generation will be in charge.

That is the custom of the manor, as it has been for a very long time. The lawyers far off in London take quite a different view. In strict legal theory Godric is only a tenant at will, who might be dispossessed at any Michaelmas when his crop has been harvested, and after he is dead his lord might give his holding to any stranger who is willing to work it. But if the lord, or his steward, tried to do anything of the kind there would be passive resistance from all the other villagers, and very soon the villagers would win. A manor can be cultivated only so long as all the peasants are broadly contented with their lot. The lord has no professional police at his disposal.

The root of the trouble is these foreign languages again. Lawyers write in Latin, and they are beginning to suppose that *villanus* equals *servus*. Now *servus* is the Latin for slave, though it may also be translated serf. And of course, a slave can have no rights against his master. The lord might take Godgifu's iron pot, or all Godric's pigs. He might order Godric to plow on the demesne for six days in the week (the Church will step in if the lord tries to make any peasant do servile work on a Sunday). "A slave can have no property that does not belong to his master." "A slave cannot know in the morning what work he must do that day." The lawyers are quite clear on these points. But the custom of the manor is opposed to them, and if it comes to a collision the custom of the manor always wins.

Besides, the lord does not want a lot of slaves. The single slave who plows the demesne is already an embarrassment. The clergy are always reminding the lord that the ownership of a slave is a grave responsibility, that in the next world he may be held responsible for any sins he has compelled his slave to commit, that to free a slave is a recognized work of mercy. If that does not appeal to the lord, there is the stronger argument of fashion. In France all the slaves have been freed; to own slaves in England is to be very out of date and provincial. When this slave gets past his work he will be freed, and the steward will pay regular wages to some freeman who will look after the demesne oxen as a full-time job.

Within a few years the village will be in the condition the Normans think proper: a great many more or less equal peasants to do the physical work, a few free men to act as clerks and managers, and one lord. Three classes instead of the innumerable ranks of English life.

Young Godric expects to follow exactly in his father's footsteps. At sixteen he cannot yet be reckoned quite a man, but next year he will put childhood away. Then the whole family will find life much easier. In payment for the holding, the steward demands the labor of one man, so that young Godric may turn out as his father's deputy. Old Godric may take an occasional day off, as his rheumatics begin to trouble him. A spare man about the place will give everyone a chance of a holiday. As time goes on young Godric will take over more and more responsibility, until his father potters among the vegetables or sits in the sun all day long.

Or, if the family feel energetic, they may extend the family holding. Even in southern England there is plenty of land to spare. What is valuable and scarce is cleared land, under cultivation. The steward will gladly allow them to grub up an acre or two of waste, which they may hold from the lord by paying a rent in money. When old Godric is past work they may not feel able to cope with this additional assart, but then some thriving cottar will probably be eager to buy it from them. There is a rhythm in these matters, as in the life of wage earners at the present day. When the children grow old enough to earn man's wages the family prospers; as the elders retire and grandchildren come along, they feel the pinch.

When young Godric is old enough to do a man's work, he will begin to look for a wife. He will have a fairly wide choice—any peasant girl from the village, or perhaps one from some neighboring village if he has the spare time to walk over and court her. It will be much more of a love match than if they were in a higher station in society; neither his parents nor hers will do the choosing for them. But it will not be entirely a love match. Even if young Godric does not fall in love, he will have to marry someone, and the girl will also be looking for a mate. There is no room in the village community for old bachelors or spinsters. Every man who works in the field must have some woman to take care of his house, and presently his mother will be too old for the task. There ought to be young children to do the odd jobs, and if young Godric has the misfortune to be childless he will be kept very busy. The family is the unit, well able to support itself; but the last members of a dwindling family will have a hard time in old age.

But if all goes well, and young Godric has children to come after him, his life will be pretty secure. He will have a full holding in the village field, and perhaps an assart as well. He will have to work for his living, but he will live well. That is, so long as the weather does its duty and the King keeps a firm peace.

Those are high matters, which affect all peasants but which peasants cannot affect. Young Godric has not lived through a famine, but he has heard stories of them. If there is not enough rain in winter, if there is too much rain in summer, if a great storm strikes while the grain is standing high, the field may yield very little. The various dodges you try then have been handed down from the ancestors. The great thing is to stay by the land. When all the grain in the village has been eaten you will be tempted to wander away; the monasteries in Winchester are generous to the starving poor, if too many other starving poor have not got there before you. But if you do not plow your holding in the winter, the steward may give it to someone who will, and then you will be a pauper until you die. No, during a famine you must hold on to your land. Probably the steward will let you fish in the lord's stream. There are various weeds which can be eaten; they will not exactly nourish you, but they will not poison you either. With berries and nuts and mushrooms you may struggle through the year, but you had better not steal the lord's game in the woods, because he will be expecting that and will be on the lookout for it. Of course, it is never worth while to poach the King's deer; it is better to die of hunger than to have your eyes gouged out with a knife.

Early in the reign of good King Edward there was a terrible famine. The price of bread rose to a fantastic height, and that bread was imported from France because there had been no harvest in Wessex. The burgesses of Winchester, who must always buy their bread, suffered dreadfully. But the dearth endured for only one year, so the village managed to survive; any peasant can go hungry for just one year at a time. That was the last of the great famines, and it was fifty years ago and more. But another may come at any time. Until the Loaf of Lammas lies on the altar one can never be sure of a harvest.

Against the other danger, war, there is no defense. One can only pray that the warriors will soon go away to fight in another part of the country. Friendly warriors just take all the food they want, without paying for it, and move on as soon as there is no more food in the village. Foreign raiders burn and slay in addition. Peasants never try to defend themselves against raiders—which is odd, since a few centuries ago their ancestors took this land by the sword. But nowadays there is a complete divorce between the swordsman and the plowman; no peasant ever carries arms, no warrior would do useful work with his hands.

There is the further complication that the village is considered part of the wealth of its lord. His private enemies may lay it waste without any personal dislike for the villagers, just to make the lord feel poorer. Of course the lord ought to defend his men, and certainly he will be fighting somewhere. But he is the lord of other manors, scattered all over England, and he may not find time to come and defend this corner of Hampshire. If armed men are seen in the neighborhood, the peasants hide in the woods until things grow quieter. No one ever dreams of resistance. The sheriff lays down that the village ought to arrest brigands, and grumbles when they run away from a few outlaws. But everyone knows the old law of King Alfred which can justify their conduct: "Seven men or less we call a band of brigands. If they are more than seven they are an army." It can never be the duty of peasants to fight an army.

Even when they are hiding in the woods from the King's enemies they must not steal the King's deer. In time of war, labor services are suspended, but nothing can excuse poaching.

Young Godric is not a pacifist; he does not think it wrong to fight. He fights with his fists against other village boys; in a serious quarrel he might use the knife he always carries in his girdle. During his own short lifetime there have been two manslayings in the village, and the hereditary feuds caused by more ancient killings are familiar features of his social background. But peasants cannot defend themselves against warriors; he takes that fact for granted, as a law of nature.

There has been peace in this part of Hampshire since the days of the mighty King Canute. Young Godric has never hidden from enemies in his life, though his father as a child took to the woods when news came that the sons of King Harold were sailing up the Channel on Viking cruise. They never came so far inland, and for nearly twenty-one years King William has kept good peace. But all the village still remembers the steep valley where the cattle should be hidden, and the dense thicket which is the best place for the sick and the young girls. A sudden rumor of alarm would get them all on the move within an hour.

Though peace has endured for so long in Hampshire, all England has heard of the merciless harrying of the Vale of York. That was the work of this King William

and his terrible Normans, and it was all the worse because he was not fighting his enemies but making a desert that his enemies would find it hazardous to cross. If
these Normans start to fight among themselves, as will
probably happen when King William dies, England will
be a bad country for defenseless peasants.

But young Godric will stay by his field. It is the only
plot of land in the whole world which he has the right to
cultivate, and to cultivate the land he sees as the proper
end of man. Warriors, pirates, outlaws—while they live
they must eat bread, and he knows how to make the land
yield bread. It is inevitable that someone will take most
of the harvest from any man who spends most of his day
at the plow, instead of capering about with a sword. If
peace should reign he will have to support his lord, and
the clergy, and those proud and dishonest burgesses in
the market town. If war comes he will have to support
someone else, between the intervals of hiding in nearby
woods. But he must stick to this task, and leave the land
in good heart to the unborn son who will work it after
him, or else the whole of Christendom will collapse.

Young Godgifu looks for the same kind of future.
Some boy in the village will marry her, or perhaps some
older man whose wife has died. Women die very easily,
perhaps more easily than men, when life is hard and
there are no trained doctors. Yet every man must have a
wife, just as every woman must have a husband. Their
existence has been planned on the basis of a family: a
strong man to work on the land, a wife to cook for him

and look after his children. A widower must soon find someone else to replace his late wife.

Young Godgifu does not expect that she will ever travel beyond sight of the village, even if trouble should come and she has to hide in the woods. She has never in her life gone so far as ten miles in a straight line. She knows that somewhere to the south is Winchester, where a bishop lives and you may sometimes find the royal court. Men from the village have been there and it is not hopelessly out of reach. In the opposite direction lies the market town. The men go there quite often, but the road is too dangerous for women unless there is a very pressing reason. Otherwise she knows nothing of England. She has heard the names of London and Gloucester, where the King occasionally stays with his court; but they are as far from her as Rouen and Paris and Rome, which she has also heard of and never expects to visit. Men from foreign parts talk in a queer way, even if you can understand what they are saying; the dialects of other parts of Wessex—Sussex and Dorset, for example—are intelligible though foreign. A man from the Midlands might as well be talking French or Latin; she will not try to grasp what he is saying. Anyway, she seldom hears such foreigners speak; her mother has taught her that a young girl ought to hide at the back of the house, or behind a bush in the field, if there are strangers about.

Her mother has taught her a great many other things, for in this remote village, lacking skilled craftsmen, every family must do everything for itself. Young Godgifu can spin both linen and wool; she would say she knows how to weave, though she does it very badly. She finds milking a cow quite easy, for the cow usually wants to be milked. To milk a ewe is harder, for they never like being handled by humans, but she can manage it. Most of the cheese eaten in the village is made from ewe's milk, and she can make that too. She helps at the butter-making, though the work is rather beyond her strength. Naturally, she keeps an eye on the hens, and notes where they lay; it is her job to feed them occasionally, when there is food to be spared. She is afraid of horses and keeps clear of the village bull, but any other animal she regards as a servant of man and will bully it and make it do what it does not want to do without a moment's hesitation. Naturally, she can also bake and brew and cook any food and keep the house reasonably clean; that is women's normal work and women are supposed to be born knowing how to do it. When she has any time to spare, she also lends a hand in the field.

With all this work to be done it is surprising that Godgifu has a private life, but she does. No agricultural work may be done on Sundays, though the animals must be fed. After Mass the villagers have the rest of the day to themselves. It is pleasant to ramble in the waste on a sunny afternoon, and the boys may pair off with the girls of their choice so long as everyone is home before dark. In a few years' time some boy or man will ask Godgifu to marry him; she cannot do the asking herself. But there are ways of encouraging a boy of her choice, or shutting the mouth of a tiresome man.

At work and at play, the young girls of the village generally keep together in a group. And when they are together they sing together. Singing is the only art they can enjoy. They cannot read because there is no one to teach them, they cannot embroider because the materials are too expensive, but they all sing. Remember the opening lines of "The Flowers of the Forest":

> I've heard them lilting, at our ewe milking,
> Lassies a' lilting before dawn o' day . . .

That comes from a much later epoch, but it was also true of the eleventh century. If they are not working while they sing, they can dance to their own music. A song that is also a dance is known as a carol—a French word, but many carols were sung in English. On the morning of a great feast, while they are waiting for Mass to begin, the whole village dances a carol outside the church door. There is a cautionary tale of a village priest who joined in a particularly secular carol just before Mass, so that the tune was still running in his head when he approached the altar. Instead of chanting the Introit, he continued with this very popular love song. But popular music is quite all right for respectable lay folk.

So although she is never idle, young Godgifu leads an intense social life. To us her future may seem dull—marriage and babies in the village where she was born, no chance of travel or of new experience. But it is the life most people have led since mankind first learned how to till the soil. If we look to a different kind of life, we are the exceptions.

Godric has provided an assured future for his elder son

and his only daughter. But his younger son, Godmund, will have to find a place for himself in the world. All the business arrangements of the eleventh century assumed a static population, or perhaps one that fell. Land itself was not very valuable, though of course someone would have rights of some kind in it. In England at that time there was no unowned land, *terra nullius*, except perhaps along the Scottish or Welsh Marches. But land with a peasant to cultivate it was precious, and that includes all the land in the village field. Godric has a full holding, which he is not likely to increase. It will go after his death to his elder son. Godgifu will marry and keep house for someone else with a full holding. Godmund cannot expect an inheritance.

There are a number of ways in which he might earn a living without leaving his native village. There is always work for a day laborer, to help some other peasant or to work in the demesne. The pay is adequate, but only so long as he works regularly; it will be hardly enough to support a wife and children, and there will be nothing in reserve for sickness or any other misfortune. If he lives to be too old for regular work there will be nothing for him but to beg at the church door. Even worse than that, to a boy of his ancestry, will be the fall in social status. If he holds no land of his own he can have no voice in the manor court, no standing in law. His equals will be the sons of slaves who were freed in their old age.

So although working for wages will be the easiest way, since he already knows how to do the work he will be hired to do, it is the last way he would choose, a desperate choice to keep from starvation. Probably he could get permission to clear an assart in the waste. That is desperately hard labor, and for the first two or three years he would gain no harvest worth speaking of and depend on his parents to feed him. He might thrive in the end, if he stuck to it; at least he might find a wife to share his hardships and have children to support his old age. It will be a life of continual hard work and at the end of it he will be barely above starvation level. That also will mean a drop in the social scale. His companions will be other landless men, beginning at the bottom. Only if he is exceptionally lucky will he be able to bring under cultivation a holding which will make him equal to the other peasants who have a full share in the village field.

The village supports only four specialists: the miller, the smith, the swineherd, and the shepherd. The miller's job is a plum, hopelessly out of Godmund's reach. There is a watermill on the village stream, where all the grain in the village must be ground. The miller has to be there all the time, to keep an eye on his revolving stones and see that his millwheel is working properly, but you hardly ever see him sweat. The village does not regard what he does as real work, and nobody likes him. He is paid with a proportion of the grain he grinds, and it is taken for granted that he cheats in the division. A share of what the miller gets goes to the lord's steward, and the steward sees that the miller has a monopoly. So the miller counts as an officer of the manor, perhaps a little superior to all honest peasants. But the present miller, a fairly decent man who does not cheat quite so blatantly as some of his colleagues, has a son who will come after him because he knows the business. That son will have to pay fairly heavily for the right to take over from his father; if by any chance the steward does not like him, the right to work the village mill will be put up to auction. But in any case Godmund, with no land and only the portion of a younger son, will never have enough money to bid for it.

It is no use trying to be a smith. Smiths form almost a hereditary caste. The present smith knows a number of useful spells, useful not only for working in iron but to stop bleeding from a wound and to take away headaches. He learned them from his father, who learned them from *his* father; they may date back to the time before the English were Christian. As it happens the present smith has no children, which may be a divine judgment on someone so mixed up with magic. But he has adopted a young cousin and is teaching him the craft. It would be absurd for the son of a plowman to take over a smithy.

There remain the two keepers of animals. They are paid by holdings in the village field, which are cultivated for them by the rest of the village or perhaps by members of their family. Though they seem to be busy all day they never plow, and to a plowman only work on the land counts as real work. So they are considered to lead idle though useful lives. Godmund knows quite enough about swine to be able to look after them, and the son of the present swineherd does not wish to succeed his father. If Godmund were offered the job in a few years' time, he would jump at it.

But he is very unlikely to get it. The swineherd, and

the shepherd also, are appointed by vote of the manor court, and they are both posts that a great many people would like to hold. For years many peasants have been canvassing and intriguing to get such a pleasant job for one of their sons, but Godric was not one of them. He has a tiresome prejudice against making even his younger son a servant to the whole village community; he believes that such a post must be vaguely derogatory. The prickly English consciousness of status enters into every transaction. Sometimes Godmund finds his father's pride rather a trial, though without it his father would be quite another person. Anyway, if his own father will not vote for him as one of the community servants, he has no chance of being elected. He has made up his mind to make a clean break and go off to foreign parts.

Even his father's pride will not be offended if he takes service directly under the King of England. As a peasant he is, of course, quite unfit to bear arms, and such a desperate course has never entered his head. To be a professional fighting man seems little better than to be a Danish pirate, and the Danish raiders are still remembered in the village as something like devils. He does not fancy being a scullion in a royal kitchen, though by all accounts royal scullions lead soft lives. That is status again. To work in a kitchen is to do the characteristic work of a slave, and there have never been slaves among his ancestors. But not very far away, measured in miles, there are servants of the King who live independently.

All the villagers have heard of the foundation of the New Forest, on the way to Winchester. The clergy, even their own parish priest, preached that it was a wicked deed, because it destroyed a few parishes. Perhaps it was a wicked deed, though not nearly so wicked as the wasting of the Vale of York. The villagers were not very shocked, partly because what became the New Forest had never been densely inhabited, partly because the people who lived there were foreign Jutes, not true West Saxons like themselves. The New Forest remained something new, as indeed it remains to this day; but to Godmund and his contemporaries it was something older than themselves, something they were used to, not a recent Norman atrocity.

The story goes, as Godmund hears it, that the King cleared it too thoroughly, and that he still wants foresters to police it. When he is old enough Godmund would like to move a few miles south and become one of these foresters. That is direct service of the King, an honorable form of service, and one open in its lower forms to native Englishmen.

It has long been settled law that anyone who harms a deer wrongs the King. King William has kept that law, and, as with all the other old English laws, he enforces it far more strictly and has made the penalties for breaking it much heavier. This last does not greatly affect peasants, and in fact many of them prefer the stricter Norman justice. In the old days the penalty was a fine, and outlawry if you could not pay up. That favored the rich, though even a rich man would be ruined if he broke the King's law too often. That was true even of manslaying. A rich man would pay the *were*, the value of the dead man, and the *bote*, the fine for breaking the King's peace. A poor man would be hanged. Nowadays King William has abolished capital punishment, though the blinding and other mutilations which are inflicted instead of hanging normally end fairly soon in death. But the punishment for killing one of the King's deer is the same as for killing a man. For a long time that has been true.

Godmund likes to wander in the woods whenever he is not scaring birds or doing some boring agricultural work. If he is accepted by the King's head forester, who is, of course, a Norman, he will be given a hut in the New Forest where he will look after a particular herd of deer. Deer are in theory wild animals, but they need as much looking after as pheasants do in the twentieth century. It will be Godmund's duty to know where his herd is feeding, to put down hay for them when the ground is covered with snow, to shoot wolves or poaching dogs or other dangerous vermin. He will carry a bow and arrows wherever he goes, and enjoy all the dignity of an armed man. If an animal of his herd gets into difficulties, it will be his duty to help it. A deer trapped in a bog must be dug out; a deer with a broken leg must be put out of its misery.

But to kill a deer, even if the killing is necessary, calls for as much formality as the execution of a man. Godmund will have to inform the King's coroner, show him the carcass and the broken leg, and depose on oath that the killing was unavoidable and performed by one authorized to do it. If he should find the unexpected carcass of a deer, he must again inform the coroner, and if the inquest leaves the death still unexplained the nearest village will be liable to a heavy fine. These are all innovations in the law, Norman innovations, naturally; but apart from these tightenings of the regulations, King William has not changed the old English law he swore to uphold. Even though he should live in the middle of the forest, Godmund will not be outside the framework of the ordinary law. He will have to join in tithing of frankpledge; if he is suspected of any crime, he will answer to the hundred court or the shire court.

He will live also under additional laws the King has introduced for the safeguarding of his forest. Godmund will not be permitted to make a clearing round his cottage, for that would be to damage the woodland. He will need a dog with a good nose to help him in his work, but that dog, like all other dogs allowed within the forest, will have to be slightly lamed by the amputation of one toe so that it cannot run down a deer by itself. Godmund himself will be subject to this additional code of law, but his main task will be to enforce it on his neighbors just beyond the boundaries of the forest. That will make him unpopular and at the same time feared. No one is very surprised if an under-forester is found lying dead in the greenwood with an arrow in his back. Then the same elaborate procedure will be followed as if he were a dead deer, and at the end the coroner will levy a substantial fine on the nearest village, though it is very unlikely that the murder will be brought home to any single man.

On the whole the neighbors do not poach deer. Everyone knows that they belong to the King, and that the punishment for harming one will be heavy. But they all think it right to cut firewood in the forest; they suppose that only an arbitrary Norman law forbids them. Godmund will have to guard the actual trees allotted to him, and that will be more difficult and make him even more unpopular.

Occasionally he may have to help with the King's hunting. The King is too busy, and too impatient, to waste time looking for a fine stag. He expects to find one waiting for him as soon as he mounts his horse. Godmund will of course keep track of any good stags among his deer, and will be expected to put the lymers on one the evening before the King hunts. Lymers are either sharp-nosed hounds on a leash, or the men on foot who lead them. They lie out all night before the King hunts, so that the real running hounds start hunting immediately. It is all very artificial, as artificial as shooting driven pheasants in the twentieth century. But the busy King can be sure of a fast and dangerous gallop through wild country, and if all goes well he will come home in a good temper. A forester who gets the King into a good temper has done a service to all the people of England.

Of course, Godmund will be under authority for the whole of his working life. What peasant is not continually under authority? But for a great deal of the time he will exercise authority over his neighbors, and be free to manage his own affairs in his own way. He will be entitled to carry arms, and people will do little services to oblige him. He may be tempted to become a petty tyrant. If he happens to be found dead no one will search very hard for his murderer. But he will have taken a step up in the world, and old Godric need never be ashamed of the career his younger son has chosen.

INDEX